HIGH SEAS HIGH RISK

The Story of the *Sudburys*

Pat Wastell Norris

HARBOUR PUBLISHING

First softcover edition 2005

Published by
HARBOUR PUBLISHING
P.O. Box 219
Madeira Park, BC, Canada
V0N 2H0
www.harbourpublishing.com

Cover painting by Harry Heine
Cover design, page design and composition by Martin Nichols
Edited by Irene Niechoda
Photos pages 103, 157 and 169 copyright Bob Sheret
Thanks to David Conn and S.C. Heal for marine editorial advice
Printed and bound in Canada

Harbour Publishing acknowledges financial support from the Government of Canada through the Book Publishing Industry Development Program and the Canada Council for the Arts, and from the Province of British Columbia through the British Columbia Arts Council and the Book Publisher's Tax Credit through the Ministry of Provincial Revenue.

Library and Archives Canada Cataloguing in Publication

Norris, Pat Wastell
High seas, high risk : the story of the Sudburys / Pat Wastell Norris.

Includes index.
ISBN 1-55017-208-5 (bound)-ISBN 1-55017-345-6 (pbk.)

1. Island Tug & Barge—History. 2. Salvage—British Columbia—History. 3. Tugboats—British Columbia—History. I. Title.
HE945.I75N67 1999 387.5'5'06571128 C99-910909-X

For Hilary and Emma

Contents

Preface

In December of 1955, the ocean-going tug *Sudbury* hit the headlines. On the front pages of west coast newspapers, black letters an inch and a half high blared: "One of the Great Feats of the Sea"; "Harbour howls, hoots, wild welcome as *Sudbury* ends epic salvage tow"; "Tug, Ship Win Epic Sea Fight." Suddenly the name *Sudbury* was familiar to all who read those papers. Blazoned across their pages, complete with hair-raising photographs, was the story of a remarkable deep-sea salvage operation.

The Vancouver Province

A Dependable Newspaper

Metropolitan Edition

very man was a hero"

CRIPPLED SHIP NEAR SAFETY

3000-mile stormy saga

B.C.'s municipal voters casting ballots today

Young hoodlums riot in city streets

Police break up mob of 100 at Robson-Seymour corner

Montreal mobs stage wild riot

The Sunday Sun

FINAL EDITION

EPIC SEA FIGHT IN PICTURES

SHOT FIRED, 5 YOUTHS FLEE

B.C. Tug Saves Ship

EXCLUSIVE PHOTOS OF HEROIC SEA SAGA

Mather's Nightcap

For twenty years the Sudburys *made headlines.* Pacific Press

For old salts, many of whom could still remember the days of sail and who now spent their days confined to recliners, or perhaps to wheelchairs, this story brought a fresh briny blast from the past. These men had struggled across heaving decks awash with water, had felt the bite of flying spume on their faces, and understood the camaraderie and humour that come with danger. The *Sudbury* became their heroine, her crew their fellows. For the Sunday sailor, the newspaper accounts reinforced the fact that the ocean is dangerous and unforgiving and that those who venture out on it fall into just two categories—the amateurs and the pros. They were a reminder that sometimes the former had no business being out there at all and that having the biggest outboard on the market didn't make you one of the latter. These, of course, were not thoughts the Sunday sailor intended to share with his wife. And for the shore-bound bank clerk, clutching a bus strap with one hand and avidly reading the paper held in the other, the drama depicted in the text and pictures activated the Walter Mitty that is in us all. Perhaps he should chuck it all, go down to the docks (wherever they were) and sign on as one of the *Sudbury*'s crew.

Even my father, who operated his own tug, put down the paper and remarked to his engineer, "And we think we have it tough, Jim."

The feat they were all reading about was the rescue of the *Makedonia*. This remarkable salvage job earned Island Tug & Barge of Victoria worldwide credibility as a salvor, as well as a huge financial return. The company's owner, Harold Elworthy, had his own notable story that was pure Horatio Alger—the classic story of a boy who started with nothing and rose to the top as a result of his own hard work and business acumen. By salvaging the *Makedonia*, Island Tug's management had, characteristically, taken a risk that paid off handsomely.

Harold Elworthy and his sons continued to demonstrate the courage to follow their hunches. They correctly concluded that the post-war years would be a boom time for deep-sea tugs. Until then, the lucrative work for BC coast towing companies was the business of moving wood. But the post-war years brought deep-sea towing opportunities. Ships that were reaching the end of their useful lives by the 1940s had been pressed into wartime service and these decrepit old hulks were still plying the seas. And the ships built during the war had been hastily constructed. The war's legacy was a tired, worn merchant fleet prone to breakdowns. And the harbours on the west coast were jammed with military vessels waiting to be towed from North America to the scrapyards in Japan. So Island Tug & Barge purchased its first ocean-going tug in 1955, and three years later bought two more. Their timing was perfect.

For twenty years Island Tug's *Sudbury*, and later her namesake the *Sudbury II*, made headlines. Their salvage jobs and their long-range tows were carried out so regularly and so successfully that their company could almost claim the Pacific Ocean as its own territory. Marine salvage is a notoriously risky business in which only a few companies survive for any length of time. This small Victoria company had made it in a fiercely competitive business and had shown itself to be as good as the best in the world. It succeeded because it had the three things that salvage requires: an astute assessment of the risk and reward, seaworthy and well-equipped ships, and crews with above-average skills.

Harold Elworthy was a good businessman but, equally important, he had a gambler's instinct, and salvage is always a gamble. He had a radio phone at home as well as in his office, and one of his captains said, "I can call H.B. at any hour of the day or night. He loves salvage. At any hour he's in there like a burglar."

Island Tug had fine deep-sea ships, ideally designed for the job and equipped with the best that money could buy. The company asked their crews what they needed and then supplied it. And finally, the crews were composed of outstanding men who could cope with anything and did. Their respect for each other was boundless. Today, more than forty years later, their pride and esprit de corps still surge to the surface. Before I could know all this, however, I first had to find these men, and that wasn't easy.

I grew up on a tugboat—quite literally. My father owned a small sawmill on the BC coast, and its assets included a 60-foot tug and several scows. Before I could walk I was carried down the dock's long ladder to be part of the crew, and as I grew, so did my responsibilities. I stood on a stool so that I could see the compass and I learned to steer a course; I ran the winch and loaded and unloaded lumber; I learned how to start the big diesel with compressed air; and I learned *not* to stand in the bight of a line. I watched others grinding valves and timing the engine, rigging up the towing gear and unshackling boom chains. I learned that when we were out in Queen Charlotte Strait and the telegraph clanged from Full Ahead to Half Ahead and then to Slow Ahead it was because we were taking what my father called "green water" over our bows. We all hung on then and we didn't talk much.

By the 1950s I had left that life and was living in the city. Even in cities few people had television in the early '50s so our news came via the daily newspapers. And month after month, year after year, it seemed, the newspapers were filled with the daring exploits of two tugs: the *Sudbury* and the *Sudbury II*. My background gave me some idea of what it took to accomplish what they did—consummate seamanship and, as Jim Derby said of Steve Fairhurst, "lots of guts."

A rare occurrence: both Sudburys *working together.*
Gordon Whittaker photo, Seaspan

Forty years later—a generation later—few remembered the *Sudburys*' achievements. These ships and their crews had lived a great adventure, but by the 1990s it was as if it had never happened. Aside from a few tattered newspaper clippings, no record of their exploits remained. Behind those old newspaper headlines, however, there were real people and I set out to find them. It was a difficult search for these voyages had all happened a long time ago and the trail was becoming cold. The company, of which these men were so proud, was no longer in existence; all the company's salvage records had been destroyed; many of the participants were dead. There seemed nothing left but those files of old newspapers. But persistence pays. Slowly, laboriously, like a detective investigation, my efforts proceeded. I advertised in magazines and a newsletter; I wrote to Lloyd's of London; my long distance telephone bills soared; Seaspan's archivist went out of her way to help; I perused miles of microfiche for names. Slowly, one small lead led to another, and then another. The people I wanted to meet, that I hoped were still around, emerged one by one and I was welcomed into universally immaculate homes and given tea, coffee, cake, tarts and sandwiches. I plugged my tape recorder into dozens of different outlets and the stories flowed into it.

Having grown up on a tugboat I thought, when I began, that I knew all about them. I was wrong. I was to learn a lot.

I was introduced to the existence of the "black gang"—the engineers, firemen and oilers whose occupation covered them with grease and oil, and I came to understand the isolation of their job down there in the bowels of a ship.

I was familiar with heavy-duty diesel engines but not with Cooper-Bessemers in particular. By the time I was finished I knew more than I ever wanted to know about these engines and could toss around the term "7,000 psi" with the best of them.

I learned something about steam engines, too: I learned that they were quiet and I learned what causes them to blow up (lack of water and a drunken watchman).

When one captain deeply mourned the loss of his cook (he didn't die, but fell overboard twice while under the influence and had to be sent home), I felt this to be an exaggerated reaction but

I came to realize that it wasn't. Cooks figured prominently in the stories I was told. There were good cooks, bad cooks, dirty cooks, drunken cooks and at least one outstanding cook.

I found that people accustomed to recording their activities precisely in a log are equally precise in conversation. So my informants felt it necessary to supply latitude and longitude. They provided exact times, and when they couldn't remember exact days they apologized. Considering that the events they were recounting had happened thirty or forty years before, an apology seemed hardly necessary.

I learned what a Senhouse slip was and I learned that a 3/8-inch steel pipe connected to a tank of propane will cut through a 12-inch shaft in no time at all.

Most important of all I learned why these people were so proud of themselves and their company.

These are their stories—their voices.

Acknowledgements

Without the help of the following people and institutions, this book would not exist. Thank you for making it possible for me to tell the story of the *Sudbury*s.

In alphabetical order you are:

Alf Armitage; Ann Blagborne; Beverly Bruce; Captain Adrian Bull; Bill Cadwalader; Duncan Cameron; Jane Carson; Captain Tim Cary; Captain Fred Collins; Nels Combe; Ed Creed; Peter Davies; Captain Jim Derby; Jake Derksen; Don Elworthy; Mark Elworthy; Rene Fournier; Captain Buster Fransvaag; Ed Gait; Terry Garraghan; Captain Alan Gray; Bob Gray; Ron Green; Norman Hacking; Captain Gary Hall; Jacques Heyrman; Glyn Holme; Captain Dave Hood; Captain Don Horn; Captain George Hunter; Lloyd's Guildhall Library, London; Peter McAllister; Captain Bob MacDonald; Leonard McCann and Joan Thornley of the Vancouver Maritime Museum; Captain Mike McQuarrie; Captain George Matson; Malcolm Mead-Miller; Norma Penhall; Tom Penway; John Perdreil; Les Rimes; Captain Robbie Robinson; John Rodgers; Amy Rolston; Harry Sapro; Ray Sundby; Debbie Tardiff and Kelly Francis of Seaspan; Captain Ray Thomas; Captain Allan Todd; Pete Van de Putte; Ray Vose; Captain John Watt; Captain Hill Wilson; George Winterburn; Peter Wright; Paul Zinkit of Columbia Sentinel Engineering, Seattle.

CHAPTER I

H.B.

"It's very rare to meet a person who has such a profound impact on you."

Harold Elworthy seems to have burst upon the world with all the talents, traits and drive that it takes to become an entrepreneur. From some remarkable gene pool he inherited the ambition, acumen and tolerance for risk that propelled him toward his goals.

Fred Elworthy, Harold's father, was born in England but like many of his young countrymen he was eager to see the rest of the world. He travelled to India and then to Ceylon, where he became manager of a tea plantation; but even this exotic locale wasn't enough to satisfy his thirst for adventure. So he bought passage on a ship that would eventually land him in San Francisco and from there, in 1885, he journeyed up the coast to the booming city of Victoria. Here, in this most English of Canadian cities, he finally settled. He became secretary of the Victoria Chamber of Commerce, a position that involved promoting BC and its industries worldwide, and he married the daughter of one of the city's pioneer families. He and his wife, the former Clara Richardson, raised four children. They christened their youngest, born in December 1901, Harold Barrington.

In the early 1900s Victoria was an ideal place to grow up; it was a small pleasant city that felt itself to be very much a part of the British Empire. The twenty-fourth of May was, indeed, the queen's birthday and it was celebrated with due pomp. There was always a parade led by a May Queen wearing royal purple and an elaborate crown; there were pipers and flower-covered floats; there was the naval band from Esquimalt and a phalanx of ratings. This impressive display was greeted with a small rustle of Anglo-Saxon applause. Victoria's citizens could lay down their lives for their country but they found it difficult to cheer for it.

H.B. Elworthy, founder of Island Tug & Barge, c. 1960. Seaspan

Aside from those few young men who went away to university or the many who left to fight in World War I, the young tended to stay in the city of their birth. Harold Elworthy was too young to serve in the war, and when he left high school there was no talk of a profession, no thought of university. Instead, at the age of sixteen, he applied for and got the job of office boy for The Pacific Salvage Company.

The Pacific Salvage Company was not as grand as its name implied but this turned out to be an advantage for its newest employee. Its modest size made it possible for him to become familiar with every facet of the business, which he did in short order. For Elworthy was where he belonged—in the corporate world—and he took to it like the proverbial duck to water. He was surrounded by things that stimulated his interest. During his lunch hour he took his brown bag and ate his sandwiches on the docks, where he could meet and talk to the crews of the tugs moored there. Why did they spend so much time tied at the dock?

he wanted to know. Where did their business come from? Who owned the companies they worked for?

One Sunday, alone in the office, Harold Elworthy received a message requesting help for a vessel in distress. The company's owner, Arthur Burdick, couldn't be found so Harold, still in his teens and having no real authority, acted quickly and decisively. Successful salvage companies *must* act quickly, often before all the facts are in. Perhaps Harold knew this intuitively; it was certainly a pattern he would follow for the rest of his business life. He ignored the unknowns, didn't wait for a contract and took it upon himself to order out one of the Pacific Salvage tugs. This first experience, however, could not be termed a complete success. At the end of the day when Mr. Burdick appeared and found that Elworthy had committed the company to a salvage operation without authorization, he fired him.

When Elworthy went into his office the next morning to clear out his desk, however, his employer seemed more kindly disposed toward him.

"Harold, my boy, what do you think you're doing?" he said, clapping his erstwhile employee on the back.

"I'm clearing out my desk."

"Don't think of it," said Mr. Burdick. "That salvage job that we did yesterday was the most profitable business we have ever done. If you get a similar call at any time in the future you do exactly what you did yesterday, and my congratulations!"

Harold Elworthy remained at his job and, within the limited scope of the Pacific Salvage Company's hierarchy, was promoted—which was a welcome development, because by the age of twenty he was married and a father. He applied his not inconsiderable talents to his job and the outcome was predictable: by the age of twenty-three he was manager of the company. Harold Elworthy was fiercely ambitious, and he wanted nothing less than ownership. But there was an obstacle to his career advancement. Arthur Burdick had a son, so there seemed to be no real future in Pacific Salvage for an "outsider." Harold turned his attention instead to one of the tugs he had visited during his lunch hours. The little *Quinitsa* spent more time at her moorings than she did towing. Harold questioned her two owner-operators.

"Can't get any work," they explained.

"I can get you lots of work. If I can keep you supplied with work would you be interested in going into business with me?"

"Sure."

The deal was struck. Harold Elworthy's savings, $500, became their working capital and, on Friday, February 13, 1925, the three partners moved into the old buildings on the former Hudson Bay dock and Island Tug & Barge was born. Immediately the *Quinitsa*, now renamed the *Island Planet*, left Victoria on the company's first job: towing a scowload of coal from Nanaimo.

Setting up their office and fuelling the *Island Planet* had depleted the new company's slender resources; until they were paid for their first tow Elworthy had exactly $125 in his corporate pocket. But he was as good as his word; he kept a steady stream of work coming their way and the business prospered. Within a very short time he had bought out his partners. Now he continued to underbid, outperform and eventually capture the business from several other small towboat men. When their businesses collapsed he offered them a job for life, and many of them accepted. But, as one of his captains said, "It's not quite the same is it?"

The towing establishment in Victoria was not particularly happy to have this young upstart in their midst but neither did they see him as a threat. "In a year or two we'll have run the young bugger out of business" was the comfortable prediction voiced over a table in the Union Club. If they weren't worried, they should have been. Prowling the docks, Elworthy had learned a great many things, chief among them that to make money, boats had to be kept busy. He kept the *Island Planet* so busy that there was barely time to refuel her. He was relentless in his pursuit of business, and business continued to come. His crews worked non-stop. Finally one of his engineers took his boss aside and filled him in on the limitations of the internal combustion engine. "You know, this engine isn't going to run forever without an overhaul," he said. "And heaven help us if it ever breaks down because you've got us booked up from now till the Second Coming."

The principals at Gardner Towing commented on the situation, as well. "See, you've got a new company," they said to Elworthy. "If your equipment breaks down don't expect our help."

"They made it very easy for me," said Elworthy years later. "They solved my problem right there." He offered Gardner $75,000 for the company and then he sought out financing. Royal Trust agreed to put up 20 percent of the purchase price and Elworthy was able to supply another 40 percent himself but, still short, he decided to approach his former employer. Pacific Salvage's Arthur Burdick agreed to supply the missing 40 percent. And so in 1926, just a year after its founding, Island Tug & Barge bought out Gardner Towing.

The large towboat owners of the day ran exemplary companies, and now Harold Elworthy joined their ranks. He had started with one little tug, a scow and a launch; twelve years later he had eleven tugs, forty scows and seven barges. He had proven that he could drum up business and he displayed another, equally important talent. Towboating is a capital-intensive business. Not only does management entrust expensive equipment to its employees, it depends on them to complete each job successfully against often formidable odds. Harold Elworthy understood right from the start that the success of his business depended, in large part, on its employees. He valued them highly and he let them know he valued them. He picked the best men he could find and then he inspired them. Applied to a lot of rough, tough tugboat men, "inspired" may seem a ten-dollar word. But there is no other word for the esprit de corps that developed. Elworthy was not to be trifled with but he treated his employees with courtesy and consideration, and in return received their respect and their unswerving loyalty. His nickname was their backhanded compliment. Publicly his employees always addressed him as Mr. Elworthy; behind his back they called him by his initials. "H.B.," they explained with affection, stood for Hard-Boiled.

Peter Wright, the company's insurance broker, was witness to the extraordinary bond between Harold Elworthy and his employees. "He was a dignified man," said Peter, "and he commanded admiration from us all. Once a month he and I toured the operation. He had perhaps seventy-five employees at the time and he greeted every one by name. He took a personal interest in their health, their families, their problems. People loved to talk to him, to work for him. It's very rare to work with a person who makes such a profound impact on you. I always tried to model myself after him."

Peter saw another side of Elworthy as well. In the early 1950s, when Island Tug's operations were in Vancouver as well as Victoria, its owner, in order to be fair, split its insurance business between brokers in both cities. The Victoria company insured the non-marine assets and Dale & Company, Peter's employer, handled insurance on the fleet. One morning, when Peter arrived for one of his regular visits, Harold Elworthy pulled out a letter and said, "Peter, I'd like you to have a look at this letter and give me your opinion."

It was a letter of declination of claim. In other words, the underwriter had turned down the claim. Having read it, Peter asked to see the form of insurance and studied it carefully.

"What is your honest opinion, Peter?" said Elworthy.

"Mr. Elworthy, I think this claim should be covered under the terms of this policy."

"Thank you very much," said Elworthy. He went over to his file cabinet, took out all the policies from the Victoria broker and laid them on the desk in front of Peter. "I'd like you to look after all those insurances," he said.

And that was that.

For Peter, a young man, it was the largest amount of business he had ever been given. Somewhat dazed, he went back to Vancouver and pursued the claim which was duly paid.

Arthur Burdick and Harold Elworthy had always been on the best of terms. Indeed, Elworthy had named his first child after his former employer. They had parted amicably when Elworthy left to start his own business and, when he needed money to expand, Arthur Burdick had supplied it. But in 1941, without Elworthy's knowledge, Burdick bought out Royal Trust's share of the business. As majority shareholder he became its self-appointed president. Elworthy, a minority shareholder in his own company, was classified as manager. Although Burdick made vague and extravagant promises about allowing his manager to buy more shares, nothing materialized, and when Elworthy asked for a raise Burdick refused him. He was not about to give the goose that laid the golden egg any further share in the profits. Mr. Burdick had just made the mistake of his life.

Once more an employee, albeit a shareholding one, Harold Elworthy had hit one of the very few lows in his life. Discouraged and disillusioned, he came close to floundering. He had two important things going for him, however: he had a wife with a remarkably strong character and friends with money and connections. Myrta Elworthy had shouldered most of the responsibilities of bringing up their four children in order to leave her husband free to pursue his business goals, and she wasn't about to see their combined efforts come to naught. And Elworthy's connections put him in touch with Stanley McKeen in Vancouver. In 1941 the two became partners and formed a new company: Straits Towing & Salvage of Vancouver. Mrs. Elworthy, who had fully supported her husband's decision to leave Island Tug, was somewhat taken aback when he decided to leave Victoria as well, and it was some time before she could bring herself to move to the "dangerous" city of Vancouver.

Harold Elworthy now found himself in competition with his former company—a company in which he still held shares. Burdick, on the other hand, had a company he knew nothing about and couldn't run. Within months of Elworthy's leaving, Island Tug & Barge's revenues sagged precipitously and within a year, Straits Towing, in partnership with Foss Towing of Seattle, bought Burdick out. It wasn't until the deal was actually formalized and Burdick was signing over his assets that he realized they included his beloved Chrysler New Yorker. He was dismayed to find that his former employee now owned not only his company, but his car.

Both Island Tug and Straits prospered. Five years after the partnership was formed, McKeen expressed interest in buying out Foss, and Elworthy took the opportunity to go his separate way. He was now in a position to regain control of Island Tug and Stan McKeen took over Straits.

Once more Harold Elworthy was off and running. Expansion of the company had always been one of his primary goals. So, in 1952, Island Tug bought the Young & Gore Towing company from Lloyd Gore. Arthur Elworthy, H.B.'s eldest son, was now vice-president of the company and he negotiated the deal. It was completed just as H.B. was leaving for a holiday in Hawaii. "Damn it all, Art. You've just ruined my holiday," he said. "That's all I'll be able to think about all the time I'm away."

It was a tribute to both principals that the deal was concluded with nothing more than a handshake. Not only that, the Elworthys had purchased a fleet that they had never even inspected. Given the reputation of the firm's owner, an inspection seemed unnecessary and, as Elworthy pointed out, seeing him poking around the Gore tugs would only have alerted his competitors.

By the mid-1950s, Island Tug had twenty-seven boats, ranging from small harbour tugs to ocean-going vessels, and a full array of barges, scows and salvage equipment. It had become one of the largest, if not *the* largest, towing companies in Canada.

The word "brainstorm" was invented for people like Elworthy. Just as he had done as a boy during those early lunch hours on the docks, he continued to ask questions and mull over the answers. Not inhibited by the strictures of too much education, his mind was free to be inventive and he saw opportunity everywhere. His staff were used to H.B.'s constant questions—"Do you think we could do this?... that? Investigate it"—and this probing encouraged their own creativity. Once an idea was termed feasible he left the details to the competent men around him and the results were invariably innovative. For instance, in 1947 Island Tug won the contract to deliver six small US Army tugs to Buenos Aires. His competitors bid on the basis of six separate deliveries, but Elworthy and his team had a different plan. They placed each tug in a specially built cradle. Then they sank a large barge, floated the tugs in their cradles onto it, pumped out the barge and headed for South America. One tug, the *Snohomish*, completed this world-record 10,000-mile tow.

This seat-of-the-pants approach extended to the company's accounting. On the rare occasion that Island Tug's accountant sharpened his pencil, made countless calculations and produced a report, he was ignored. "Don't bother me with projections and all that nonsense," said H.B. Bean counters were just that, in Elworthy's opinion, and the unfortunate accountant was required to rearrange the figures on the bottom line until they met with his employer's approval.

Elworthy had always leapt ahead with breathtaking boldness. He had committed the *Island Commander* to the use of the US Army, for example, while still negotiating the purchase of Burdick's Island Tug shares. And, when he was one of the consortium that bought several war surplus corvettes and sold one of them, the *Sudbury*, for conversion to a towboat, he had already decided that one day he would own her. Island Tug was already doing some deep-sea towing and there was every indication that this business would increase in the future. Elworthy and his sons discussed this prospect. They saw a seemingly endless supply of war-weary merchant ships out there in the Pacific finding themselves in distress. Their propellers were dropping off; their engines were breaking down. And if the mechanics didn't do them in, another interesting problem did: curiously, they ran out of fuel. In one year alone, in the mid-fifties, four ships limped into Vancouver with barely enough fuel to get them to their moorings. Indeed, some of them were reduced to using their stove oil as fuel. All of them had come light from Vladivostok to load wheat for that port. And a persistent rumour circulated on the waterfront: mariners said that up in the lonely reaches of the far north Pacific they had come upon a stationary Soviet tanker—a permanent fixture, so to speak. It was surmised, although it cannot be proved, that the poorly paid crews of these merchantmen filled their tanks with as much oil as they could carry, calculated their actual requirements to the last teacupful and then sold the excess to the tanker. Those who had calculated correctly made it to the dock. The others sent out distress calls.

And so, in 1954, Island Tug bought the *Sudbury*. Within a very few years this ship and her namesake, the *Sudbury II*, would make Island Tug & Barge of Victoria known in maritime circles around the world.

CHAPTER II

The SS *Sudbury*

"After the war a lot of these little ships ended up as razor blades, but not the Sudbury*."*

The fact that corvettes existed at all was due to a miscalculation on the part of the British Admiralty. In the early 1920s and '30s the Admiralty believed that in any future war the threat to merchantmen would come from aircraft or surface vessels. In 1939, when the Germans unleashed their U-boat fleet, it became quite clear that the menace to shipping would come from *under* the water. This realization, this late in the game, resulted in a scramble for escort vessels to protect convoys and engage in anti-submarine warfare. The military cast about for something simple, suitable and quick to build.

One of the shipbuilders to submit plans was Smith Dock Co. Ltd. of Middlesbrough, England. This company built trawlers and whale-catchers, and their representative argued, reasonably enough, that a ship that was built to hunt whales would be equally adept at hunting submarines. The vessel's purpose dictated an exceptional manoeuvring ability—it could change direction in a matter of seconds—and it had a simple, reliable steam engine. It was decided that the design of the escort vessels would be a modification of the company's whale-catcher, *Southern Pride*. The resulting ships, designated as Flower-class corvettes, were soon being churned out by shipyards in Britain, Ireland and Canada.

By 1941, the year that the HMCS *Sudbury* slid down the ways in Kingston, Ontario, the U-boat campaign was at its peak. Fully a quarter of the slow-moving merchantmen that sailed from North American ports failed to reach their destinations. The *Sudbury* and her sister ships, officially identified as Patrol Vessels–Whaler Type, became their protectors. They assumed this role under a considerable handicap: they were simply too small for the job. This handicap was due to another miscalculation on the part of the Admiralty. In the haste to get the ships into service, no one questioned that they would be used in anything but coastal waters. Yet they now found themselves taking on the brunt of the Atlantic convoy duties. At 204 feet in length they were ill-equipped to handle the huge seas of the open ocean or, as Mr. L. Woollard, MA, RCNC, put it: "Their dimensions are small in relation to those of the waves encountered." Some years later a whole troop of towboat men would come to share this opinion.

The Flower-class corvettes had a maximum speed of 16 knots which was perhaps not enough. When the ship dropped a depth charge she didn't always get away from the explosion fast enough, causing the Chief Engineer to charge up out of the engine room voicing colourfully phrased complaints that the deck officers' stupidity had damaged some of his machinery. They were "lively" little ships, which is a polite way of saying that in a sea they bucked and reared like demented broncos and, like bronc riders, their deck officers hung on for dear life and watched in awe as their ship periodically buried her nose in a wall of water and pointed her stern to the sky. They were not only lively but "wet": their short forecastle permitted green seas to thunder over the forward decks. Adding to the general discomfort was their round-bottom design, which caused them to roll fearsomely. "They would roll on wet grass," said one crew member. So they were, even the Admiralty admitted, "exhausting" ships for the crew. As a former engineer, John Henderson, remembers: "There was so much water coming down the ventilators and the skylight that we used to wear oilskins in the engine room. There was nothing to hang on to. You just hung on to anything that was handy and avoided hot pipes. It was a very unsatisfactory way of making a living."

The *Sudbury* was one of the first of these ships to be built and was to be one of the longest surviving. She was to become famous for her exploits, which would have nothing to do with war. She was to spend much of her working life in the North Pacific yet she began it in the Caribbean. Named for the gritty little mining town that supplied the war effort with nickel, she left her staid Canadian place of origin and almost immediately headed for a more exotic locale.

The Sudbury *as a corvette.* Maritime Museum of BC

The *Sudbury* was commissioned in Montreal on October 15, 1941 and arrived in Halifax on October 26. Just over a month later, the United States entered the war. The US Navy was, at that point, unfamiliar with the convoy system. It had no suitable ships to protect American merchantmen and, like the British and Canadians before them, their vessels were being lost at an alarming rate. To remedy the situation, the Canadian government loaned them escort vessels, including the *Sudbury*. She was sent to the West Indies as part of a tanker escort force and then, when her tour of escort duty was finished, she was reassigned to the run from Halifax to New York.

When she arrived in Halifax to assume her new duties she brought passengers with her—gargantuan tropical cockroaches. By the time Norman Hacking joined the ship as first officer these cockroaches had become an integral part of the crew. When not taking part in cockroach races, they gathered in the wardroom pantry where they sat on the butter and waved to the diners. Unfortunately one of them overstepped the bounds of hospitality by falling into the captain's soup. As a result of this indiscretion all of them suffered a gas attack. Cannisters of cyanide were brought aboard, all the doors and portholes were sealed, and the crew vacated the premises for forty-eight hours. When the fumigation was completed Norman was given a gas mask and the job of airing out the ship. The sight that met his eyes in the wardroom pantry was pathetic. In their frantic rush to escape the deadly gas the cockroaches had all huddled in one corner and now lay there in a heap, feet in the air. Norman proceeded to break the seal on the doors and windows and, as he did, his attention was arrested.

"Those damned cockroaches got up and stretched their legs and in ten minutes they were as lively as ever," he said.

The cockroaches had won this battle. They remained part of the *Sudbury*'s complement and no doubt their descendants went on to sail to the Aleutians.

Having conceded defeat in this area, the captain turned to a problem more easily solved—that of the ship's radar. The early corvettes were particularly ill-equipped. They had an obsolete type of asdic, no gyrocompass and no radar. The *Sudbury* had been equipped with radar but it was Canadian-made, which meant that, in those days before Canada's technological excellence had developed, it was virtually useless. So the *Sudbury* crossed the Atlantic with a convoy, had new British radar installed, and joined another convoy for the return journey. It was November 1943, and halfway through the homeward voyage a ferocious north Atlantic gale descended on the long straggle of ships.

The rest of the convoy were old hands and they hove to. Not so the *Sudbury*. Her youthful captain lacked both experience and common sense. Ignoring the example set by the other ships he chose his own course of action, action dictated by the principle of "maintaining speed." So he maintained speed. The *Sudbury*, instead of hunkering down like her fellows, made every wave a confrontation. Finally the sea decided to slap some sense into her. A wall of water hit the little ship and took off the port wing of the bridge and flooded the galley. It broke the cook's leg. It swept away the life rafts and the lifeboats. The steel Ready-Use locker that was welded to the deck disappeared into thin air.

The vessel that struggled into St. John's Harbour some days later was a wreck. She went directly to the shipyards for a refit, but even after repairs were made she was considered unfit for the rigours of the North Atlantic. Instead she was sent to the naval base at Esquimalt on the Pacific coast. Had her future crews known this part of her history, they might have been less sanguine. It was, perhaps, better that they didn't know. They would have enough to worry about as it was. Some of her future crew members *did* have misgivings about the *Sudbury*. Captain Adrian Bull said, "The old *Sudbury*—I was never happy on her. I figured she was going down almost momentarily. They would load her up with fuel and the fuel would come right up through the decks. She was very lightly built. She was built for speed. You could always get a little more speed out of her but you'd really wonder if it was worth it.

In the summer of 1945, the world was celebrating the end of the war. After all those people had lost their limbs and their lives and their loved ones, it was all over. After the mines and the torpedoes and the shooting and sinking, it was all over. And if you aren't fighting a war, warships are something of a glut on the market. A lot of them end up as razor blades.

The *Sudbury* was spared that fate. At war's end she became

one of those irresistible bargains known as "war surplus." The words "war surplus" turned a population starved for material possessions into ravening bargain hunters. Teenage boys snapped up webbing ammunition belts and water bottles and adults bought gabardine trench coats in a choice of three colours—navy, khaki or air force blue—for $25. If you had good connections the bargains were even more spectacular. In 1946 a group with just such connections bought the *Sudbury* on spec for a price that guaranteed the purchasers a handsome profit when they resold her.

The Sudbury *in her Island Tug colours.* Seaspan

Two years later Pacific Mills, a subsidiary of Crown Zellerbach, bought her and converted her into a tug. And then, in 1954, Harold Elworthy bought her for somewhere in the neighbourhood of $500,000 and put her into Yarrows for an extensive overhaul. She was given a new, higher speed towing wheel, and modern radar capable of scanning a 90-mile circle. She was outfitted with loran, an echo sounder and all manner of items for deep-sea salvage work. The detailed list of salvage equipment she now carried occupied three typewritten pages. It included the following:

2,000 feet of $1\frac{7}{8}$ inch steel towing hawser plus a spare hawser
3 - 6" self-priming pumps*
2 - 4" self-priming pumps
1 - 3" self-priming drainage pump
2 sets of diving dress C/W submarine telephones
1 air compressor
2 sets of oxygen and acetylene cutting equipment

The Sudbury *converted from corvette to salvage vessel in the 1950s.* Seaspan

1 portable welding machine
1 complete set of Cox Underwater Gun (the only complete set on the Pacific Coast)
1 underwater double-bladed power saw
1 set of pneumatic hammers & rock drills
2 complete sets of ground tackle

*By the time the *Sudburys* were dismantled and sold, they had 8-inch pumps as well. Some idea of the capacity of these pumps is made clear by the fact that they were purchased by a land developer who used them to drain a lake!

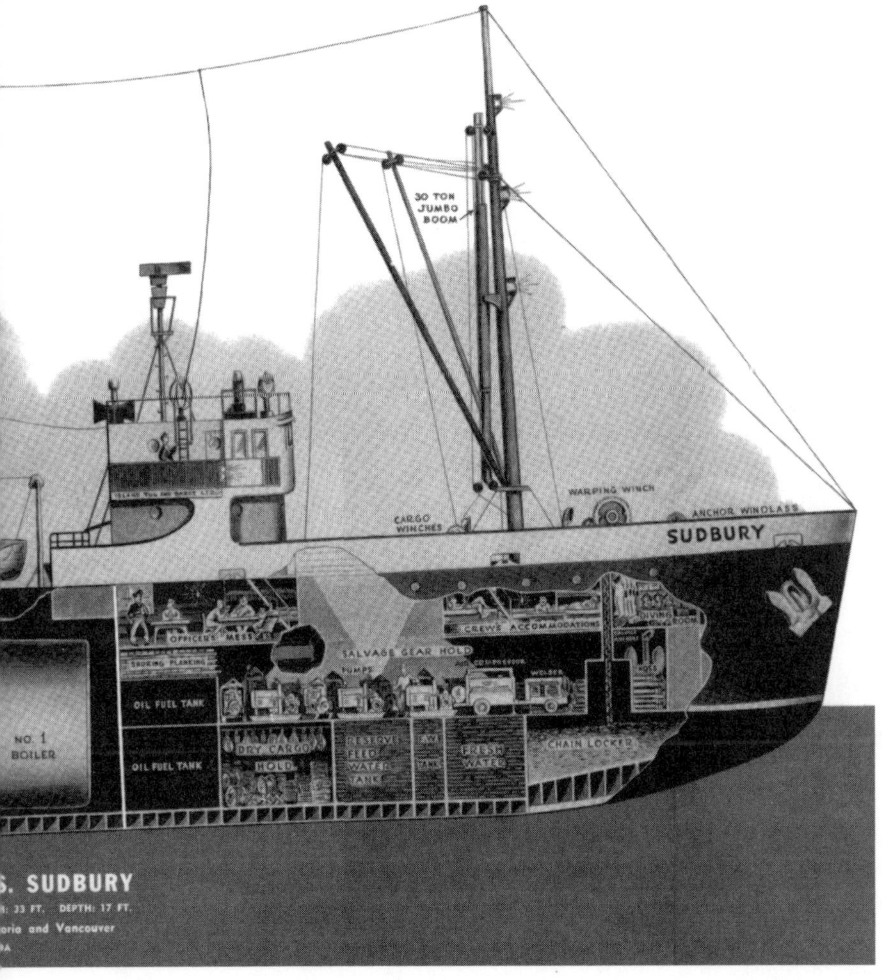

The *Sudbury*'s specs, equipment and capabilities were outlined and distributed to ships' agents and other potential customers. This advertising campaign didn't start out all that auspiciously, George Winterburn recalls. "We had a photographer on board to take pictures for the company. We had had kind of a wild night. For one thing, we blew up a generator and the ship was blacked out. This poor photographer—he wasn't impressed." H.B. was always eager to seize a fruitful opportunity for PR. Ten years later, for example, one of the *Sudbury*s was loaned to the organizers of Victoria's Swiftsure Yacht Race as a PR gesture. It was the crews' least favourite assignment. "They used to send us out on the Swiftsure Yacht Race carrying reporters," said Adrian Bull. "That was a... You never saw so many drunks in a confined space."

While Harold Elworthy waited for customers to materialize, he proceeded with his own plans for the *Sudbury*. Flat booms of logs and even Davis rafts were a thing of the past by now; logs were being moved in barges which had proven themselves to be faster, safer, cheaper transporters of wood. Elworthy had been casting about for some of these barges to add to his fleet, as the bids for building new ones had proven to be prohibitively high. He found the solution in Venezuela, of all places, where Shell Oil had three tankers for sale and Imperial Oil, one. Stripped of their superstructures they could be converted into log barges.

Elworthy conferred with Norman Turner, his marine superintendent, and they decided that their tug (or tugs, as it turned out) would go down to Venezuela and tow all four ships through the Panama Canal and up the west coast to Victoria. No one, of course, had ever attempted to do anything like this before, but that fact didn't discourage H.B. He had built his business on innovation. Whenever insurance underwriters had a salvage job that nobody else was prepared to tackle, he took it on. It was then up to his clever, competent staff to figure out how to attack the logistics. From Jake Derksen, the former high-lead logger, who had just the rigging expertise they needed, to Norman Turner, who kept a notebook filled with arcane calculations and worked out the engineering details, they could rise to meet any challenge.

In Norman Turner, Harold Elworthy had found exactly the man he needed as marine superintendent, and a good part of the company's success was due to his talents. His competence was recognized at Island Tug and, indeed, much further afield. Such was his reputation that in time, Lloyd's of London was willing to place insurance with nothing more than Norman Turner's assurance that it would be a tolerable risk. Now this remarkable man turned his attention to the longest quadruple tow anyone had ever attempted. He drew up a precise and complicated diagram for the towing gear. A series of towing wires, shackles, steel pennants and chains would connect two tugs with the four tankers following in line. The entire tow would stretch for more than a mile and the towing wires would lie 100 feet below the surface of the water. It was an original and daring procedure and they had only Norman Turner's word that it would work.

Island Tug chose Roy Blake to captain the *Sovereign* and John McQuarrie to captain the *Sudbury*, and as backup they sent along Fred McFarlane, their port captain. Among others who were hired was Ray Sundby, the *Sudbury*'s mess boy. Ray, a tall, fair Norwegian boy with beguiling blue eyes and an open smiling face, was delighted to have secured this job. He and his family had arrived from Norway just eight months previously and Ray had only been able to find casual day labouring jobs. Now he had not only permanent employment, but the promise of adventure. He assured his mother that he would send her postcards from all his exotic ports of call and he promised himself that he would keep a diary of this trip to the tropics. He was as good as his word. From day one he endured debilitating bouts of seasickness and a ship's cook who was a vile-tempered alcoholic; at every port he took pictures and in his bake-oven little cabin he learned to develop them; he fought a constant battle with the wind-catcher that periodically dumped gallons of water onto his bunk; and, in the final days of the trip, he developed a serious infection. He chronicled the whole voyage with complete candour, for he wrote in Norwegian.

CHAPTER III

The *Conchita*, the *Chepita*, the *Carlota* and the *Icotea*

"Oh my God, what is that—
looks like a train coming.
By golly, you won't believe it;
it's a tug towing four *tankers."*

In early June 1954, Island Tug's newest acquisition left Victoria harbour with almost as much flourish as did the Empress ships of old on their departures for the Orient. The crew lined the *Sudbury*'s rail to wave for the newspaper photographers and office staff and shipyard workers lined the dock to wave goodbye to the crew.

For Ray Sundby, the galley boy, the preparations for this departure began on a high note. He and the rest of the crew were flown to Vancouver to get their immigration papers in order and to get the shots that were required for a foreign voyage. It was Ray's first flight and he found it "wonderful to fly." Not so the ship's oilers, Oscar Hodne and Hans Westergaard, who were old hands. They had spent World War II in the merchant service and having survived sinkings and any number of lesser marine disasters they were not about to tempt fate further by entrusting their lives to a commercial airline. They took the ferry.

Ray Sundby, the disenchanted mess boy, aboard the Sudbury, *1954.*
Photo courtesy Ray Sundby

And Ray's euphoria soon vanished. Before they even left the dock he was serving meals, washing dishes and stowing mountains of provisions under the supervision of a permanently foul-tempered cook. When they finally did leave the harbour and emerged from the Strait of Juan de Fuca into the open Pacific, he found that seasickness compounded his problems. He started each day determined to "act like a regular seaman" but the smell of bacon, eggs and greasy fried potatoes were his undoing. His stomach, he noted in his diary, "started with a slow waltz, went into a tango, then a rumba and finally a jitterbug," at which point he would dive for the toilet. The first dive was especially memorable. A wave hit the side of the ship and a faulty valve in the toilet let in a burst of sea water which sprayed the toilet's contents all over Ray, the walls and the ceiling.

The *Sudbury* rolled on down the coast. Off the port bow the high brown line of California appeared: through binoculars the crew could see the miles of bluffs that marked the shoreline. Here and there these had collapsed into the sea, leaving gouges in the scanty vegetation and a talus slope of dusty soil.

Two or three days before they reached San Pedro, Alan Gray, the second mate, was busy at the chart table when Herb Marian, the second engineer, appeared in the wheelhouse. Before they could exchange a word Herb collapsed and as he went down he struck his face on the steel door jamb.

"What's all this about," cried Alan in dismay.

"I think he's having an epileptic fit," said the helmsman.

"Christ almighty," Alan had never seen an epileptic seizure in his life. "What do I do?"

The seizure itself was short-lived but the engineer remained unconscious and a deep gash in his face was gushing blood.

"I went down and got every Band-Aid I could get my hands on," said Alan, "and I plastered him up and then we flung him in the skipper's bunk."

John McQuarrie, the captain, had been down below. Alerted by Alan rustling through the first-aid kit, he came up to his cabin. "We'll just leave him there till he comes to," he said.

By the time they reached San Pedro, Herb had recovered. Still, as they entered the harbour, they had the flag up for the doctor and when he came on board and inspected the patient he found the Band-Aids had worked remarkably well. This was a relief for Alan, who had a confession to make.

"I didn't have the guts to stitch him up," he told the doctor.

On June 13 the ship docked at San Pedro for refuelling, and

there was time for Ray Sundby to go ashore. He found it "an awful town." Surrounded by a forest of naked black oil derricks, it was depressingly ugly. And the drinks were expensive—50 cents for a finger of gin, he complained in his diary.

It was much hotter here. Summers in Victoria were never more than warm, any real heat being dissipated by the strong cold winds off the surrounding ocean and the snow-covered Olympic Mountains. But on the coasts of southern California and Mexico the ocean was like a mirror and there were no cool breezes to blow away the heat. To make matters worse, the *Sudbury* was painted company colours: her superstructure was white, her stack red with a black band and her hull black. Like a giant radiator the hull absorbed heat during the day and radiated it into the crew's quarters all night. Jack Daly, the diver, finally abandoned his bunk below and rigged up a hammock on deck where he slept, swinging gently back and forth. Others in the crew hauled two-by-fours out of the wood room and rigged up a canvas canopy on the stern for shade.

With the heat came the first violent electrical storm. Jack Daly and his tenderman, Jake Derksen, were out on deck having a smoke when the first one hit the *Sudbury*. "You can't believe what's in those clouds," said Jake. "One minute thunder, lightning and raindrops as big as buckets were pelting down. The next minute—wham—I was lying on the deck looking up at the bottom of the lifeboat."

Jack was the first to struggle to his feet. He leaned over the prostrate form of his tenderman. "Jake," he said, "Jake, are you okay?"

Jake opened his eyes, considered the bottom of the lifeboat and tried to orient himself.

"Yeah," he said, "I seem to be okay. Don't even have a headache." Jake took things as they came. "You never know," he said. "May have smartened me up a bit."

Alf Armitage, the third engineer, was asleep in his bunk when the lightning hit; suddenly jerked to consciousness by an earth-shattering bang, he leaped for the door. "I thought we'd been bombed," he said. In the engine room the Chief, Walter Hitchen-Smith, was thrown flat on his back. In the wheelhouse the ship's navigational equipment was damaged.

"It was as if a huge storm had been let out of a bag," said Ray Sundby. "The rain didn't pour down, it flowed. Constant thunder and lightning. No space between them. The skipper ordered us not to touch any metal but I had to go up on deck and close the skylight because we were swimming in the galley. A nasty wind got up and we lost our canopy. The two-by-fours were broken off like matchsticks and then huge waves washed it all over the side. It lasted about an hour and then all was quiet as before."

The crew had to ignore the captain's somewhat gratuitous advice not to touch anything metal. There was virtually nothing on the *Sudbury*, save the bedding and the crew's clothes, that *wasn't* metal. Still, they found that there were activities to be avoided. Farther south in the Panama Canal, Carl, the third mate, had just begun to wash down the decks when suddenly a streak of fire inexplicably spewed from the nozzle of the hose. "Wha-a-a," yelled Carl, flinging the hose away from him. That put an end to deck washing.

They had been at sea for two weeks now and the tedium and the heat were wearing down both men and machines: one of the engine bearings was overheating and the freezer, used to Victoria's temperate climate, was threatening to quit; Jimmy the cook, an alcoholic, had settled into a more or less permanent hangover which did nothing to improve his personality; and the food in the dry storage room was beginning to rot, creating a smell like an open latrine. Cursing and complaining, the cook carried a ham and 20 pounds of putrid baloney to the side and threw them into the sea.

And Alf Armitage and Jack Daly had their own small altercation. As diver, Jack had no real duties while the ship was underway so he filled in his time with odd jobs, one of which was chipping paint. While Alf was trying to sleep, Jack was chipping paint—right over his head.

"I can't get any sleep with you and that fucking paint chipper," complained Alf. "Why don't you work over on the other side?"

"Naw," said Daly, "I want to work here in the shade."

"Okay Jack, you go right ahead, but remember, every dog has his day." Alf abandoned his bunk and headed for the galley.

The day arrived when Jack himself was asleep, swinging in his hammock, his head just inches from the engine room bulkhead. Alf made some careful calculations as to the position of Jack's head. Then he got a ten-pound hammer, checked his calculations and let fly at the interior of the bulkhead. Jack left his hammock as if shot from a cannon.

"Just chipping paint in the engine room," said Alf grimly.

In the Panama Canal. Ray Sundby photo

Fortunately the Panama Canal provided a diversion. In his diary Ray Sundby wrote: "Today we went through the Canal. I worked more than I have ever done in my twenty years of life. The pilot had to have his meals served in the wheelhouse and in the crew's mess were ten extra blacks—the auxiliary crew we need for going through the Canal. Fortunately one of them helped me to wash the dishes. After all, I wash dishes for nineteen men three times a day plus snacks—now I had eleven more to wash dishes for. The Canal was very impressive. They had to cut through huge mountains. I tried to go topside to take some pictures but the pilot caught me and refused to let me photograph. He said, 'The US soldiers have orders to shoot and they are just stupid enough to do so.' The Americans are very unpopular here just as they are everywhere else, one of the blacks said. They have all the best jobs, he said, and everybody else works for a pittance."

Labour *was* cheap. This was quite evident from the fact that it took two customs officers two days to measure the *Sudbury* and calculate the charges for negotiating the canal. And when Alf Armitage got an ear infection from swimming in the none-too-clean waters and had to go to the hospital for treatment, the ship's agent supplied him with a car and driver. To Alf's horror, he discovered that the man had asked the agent for $5 for his services over two days—and was beaten down to $4. Alf added another $4 to the kitty and reflected that wages like these were to blame for Panama City's crime. "It wasn't a place you'd want to wander around," he said. "You'd be just as likely to get your throat cut."

The *Sudbury* had completed the first leg of her long voyage; now she headed across the Caribbean toward Venezuela, bucking heavy seas. Across that same stretch of water, Norman Turner, Island Tug's marine superintendent, was flying to meet them. Notified of their ETA, he was waiting on the dock in Maracaibo when they arrived. A few days earlier, Turner had obtained his passport, $500 in travellers' cheques and a $2,500 line of credit, and left Victoria for South America. Physically he was on a commercial flight but metaphorically he was flying by the seat of his pants. It was he who was responsible for the success or failure of this tow—a tow that no one else had ever attempted. The plans that he had made in his office were now to be tested, modified or perhaps abandoned at the site.

After a month at sea the crew of the *Sudbury* had expected the exotic-sounding city of Maracaibo to fit their vision of a tropical paradise. Instead they found, in Ray Sundby's words, "a really filthy dump." In other parts of the city there were broad tree-lined streets flanked by Spanish-style mansions, but down by the docks the houses were little more than shacks. Daylight showed through the cracks in their walls and they looked hardly suitable habitations for pigs or chickens. Yet when Ray managed to peek into one or two of them he was astonished to see refrigerators, radios and electric irons, an indication that oil money had trickled down to the lowest level of this country's society. Even in Canadian dollars everything was wildly expensive, including the drinks, so it was a bad-tempered lot that sailed upriver into the Sea of Maracaibo.

The land around Lake Maracaibo, as it is commonly called, was low-lying and covered with scrub. Houses perched on stilts appeared here and there and marsh grass oozed out into the water. The only exotic touch was provided by the palm trees that dotted the shoreline. As in San Pedro, a forest of oil rigs rose from the surface of the water and stretched away as far as the eye could see. And the humid air was further weighed down with the thick smell of oil.

Twenty miles into this strange industrial forest the *Sudbury* came to Las Salinas and found the tanker she was looking for: a former Imperial Oil ship, the *Icotea*. She was not an impressive sight. Rust-covered and weary, she swung at anchor. The *Sudbury* came alongside and her crew prepared to face their first challenge. They had been instructed that, before attempting to tow her, they were to remove the tanker's propeller to reduce drag. In time they would become adept at this job. Jake Derksen explained the procedure: "First we secured the propeller from up top with cables, then we removed the nut holding it onto the shaft. We wrapped Primacord around the shaft and attached a fuse to it. Lit the fuse and—bam—the propeller came off just as nice as you please and we hoisted it up and onto the deck of the ship. If the nut itself wouldn't budge, we put a spanner on it and tied a charge of powder to the spanner's handle. If we had to cut through the shaft, we connected a length of 3/8-inch steel pipe to a propane tank and lit the end. Man, did that thing cut." This last ingenious arrangement would probably have induced apoplexy at the Workmen's Compensation Board but fortunately that organization was unaware of it.

Expertise was yet to come, however, and this first effort was a trial for all concerned, especially the *Sudbury*'s diver. Jack Daly put on his diving suit and dropped into the warm Venezuelan water. In no time at all he was up again, drenched in sweat, unable to work in water that temperature. So Norman Turner ordered a pump from below and pumped enough water in the forward tanks of the freighter to tilt her nose down and lift her propeller out of the water. Then Jack straddled the shaft and attacked it with an acetylene torch. After several hours and not much to show for it, Norman was exasperated. "What the hell are you doing over there," he yelled. "Are you actually cutting anything or just burning up sticks and gas?" Jack Daly stood six-feet-four and had a high opinion of his own abilities. Only Norman's exalted position in the company's hierarchy saved him from physical injury.

Jack Daly attempting to cut off the tanker Icotea*'s propeller.* Ray Sundby photo

It took another full day in the enervating heat to finish the job. Then Turner took off by plane for Curaçao and the *Sudbury* picked up a pilot and headed downriver dragging the *Icotea* behind her.

The river that flows into the Gulf of Maracaibo brings tons of silt with it, making the waters of the gulf shallow. So when the *Sudbury* rounded a corner and found herself buffeted by strong winds, the waves that had built up were ferocious. Seeing the little pilot boat beating its way out to them, the pilot prepared to depart. However as the boat got closer, appearing and disappearing behind gigantic waves and bursts of foam, it was apparent that there was no way she could actually get alongside. There was much waving and shouting in Spanish before the pilot finally faced the fact that he couldn't be taken off. He then tried another tack and attempted to persuade John McQuarrie to turn around and take him back to calmer waters.

"Are you crazy?" said the skipper. "We've got a tow. With a tow you don't turn around."

"The pilot wanted to be home to celebrate July 5th, Venezuela's Independence Day," said Alf Armitage. "He was considerably pissed off. He spent the next couple of days drunk."

The mood of the rest of the crew wasn't a lot better. The slow hot trip and the prospect of having to remove three more propellers frayed tempers. The deck crew raged at the bosun, the captain and the cook were at each other's throats, and Ray Sundby was in a fury because the wind-catcher, out the porthole above his bunk, caught a wave and drenched everything in the cabin. Ray's cabin was just above the boilers and in this tropical climate resembled an oven more than a bedroom. Every time he tried to get some air circulation he was rewarded instead by a deluge of sea water. Even in the mess room at deck level waves slapped through the ports if they were left open. A fireman, no doubt fried by the heat in the engine room, came up for breakfast and insisted on opening a porthole. "We warned him not to do it," said Ray. "But no, he knew better. No sooner had I served him than a huge wave hit the ship, came right in and landed on his plate. Eggs and bacon floating around. Not only did he make a mess of his own breakfast but also Rusty's who was sitting opposite him. He didn't say a word—just ate his wet eggs and bacon and even the toast, which was soaking."

They finally reached the huge curve of Amway Bay and anchored the *Icotea*. They were told that the pilot, who would guide them into Curaçao, would arrive at 6:00 the next morning. "Six o'clock comes and no pilot," said Alf. "Six-thirty comes and goes. 'To hell with it,' said McQuarrie, 'we're going.' Away went John. I think it cost him $5,000. You pay a fine if you go without a pilot."

With the *Sudbury* moored in Curaçao her crew drew out some cash and headed for the nearest bar where they drowned their frustrations in alcohol. Ray had a rum and Coke and two Tom Collinses which cost him ten dollars and made him feel "quite

Pete Van de Putte. In the tropics, the temperature in the engine room reached 125°F.
Ray Sundby photo, Seaspan

cross-eyed," so he left the rest to their drinks and went off in search of camera equipment. He had brought his camera and lenses with him; now he wanted to try his hand at developing his own film. He found a developing kit, wandered around sightseeing, and went back to the *Sudbury*.

In the morning it was obvious that some of his shipmates had hit the booze with more single-minded purpose than Ray had. The cook was unconscious. Among the sheets and towels in the linen room Ray found the body of a man he had never seen before. When he finally revived, this man was discovered to be a Norwegian. In his befuddled state he was fortunate, indeed, to have been discovered by a fellow countryman who could communicate with him and send him off in the general direction of his own ship. By this time the captain, severely hungover himself, had stormed into the cook's cabin and got him on his feet. Jimmy struggled into the galley, heaved several frying pans onto the stove and confided to Ray that his drinking days had come to an end. "Would you please take the rest of my beer and throw it overboard right now," he said.

God help me if I had, Ray reflected.

There was one bright spot in all of this. Norman Turner, arriving ahead of them, and no doubt disenchanted by their efforts in Las Salinas, had arranged to have the propellers removed at a shipyard in Curaçao. Her crew having been spared this task, the

Sudbury left in the early hours of July 9 and headed for Panama City. Behind her trailed the *Icotea* and a second tanker, the *Conchita*. If their progress to Curaçao had been slow it was now doubly so. Ray Sundby considered the situation with despair: we have two more tankers to pick up, Victoria is 4,000 miles away and I could probably keep up with this tug swimming, he told himself, suddenly assailed by homesickness.

In Panama both tankers were anchored and the *Sudbury* docked for repairs to her radar which gave her mess boy the opportunity to do a little sightseeing. Cheered by this break in routine, he took his camera and set off. The streets were filled with people and music. He window-shopped, haggled over prices of souvenirs and wandered into a cathedral. Its wildly rococo interior dazzled him at first and he thought it the most beautiful sight he had ever seen. But then his sense of Scandinavian simplicity asserted itself and, on second thought, he decided that it was actually "pretty tasteless."

In an effort to prevent the excesses of Curaçao, the skipper had doled out a limit of $10 to anyone who wanted to go ashore. This resulted in much muttering and complaining. However, Pete Van de Putte, one of the engineers, found a way to overcome this financial obstacle to a good time. Late in the evening Ray dropped into a bar and found Pete dancing solo on the dance floor in his socks. He was several sheets to the wind, had sold his shoes for a couple of drinks and, for the right price, was prepared to sell his pants. He was also "so noisy" that Ray left him and went back to the *Sudbury* to bed.

Up until this point, except for a few short, fierce electrical storms, they had had relatively good weather. Now that was to change. As they headed back to Curaçao to pick up the last two tankers, a full-fledged storm burst upon them, bringing with it Force 11 winds. Waves crashed over the *Sudbury* and water swept down the vents and inundated the galley stove and the dry storage room. In protest the stove shut down. Cursing the thorny path that was his life, the cook waded into the quagmire in the storage room and dragged sodden comestibles to the engine room to dry out. In the corridors, rivers of water sloshed back and forth as the ship pitched and rolled. On the stern the canvas awning had been replaced and was now held in position by metal supports. The seas tore off the canvas and bent the metal posts. Ray Sundby was prostrate with seasickness and thought longingly of drowning and ending his misery.

Jake Derksen fared better. Jake was born on the prairie and when he first joined Island Tug and found himself out in a storm on the west coast, he was not a happy man. "Me, I had no idea about water," he said. "We were out on the *Island Ranger*. There was a broom hanging on the wall in the galley and it swung around till it hit the ceiling. I thought, Oh my god, this is like being out in a rowboat. It took us three or four days to get to Zeballos and I never slept a wink."

Stormy Caribbean seas. Seaspan

The *Sudbury* fought this Caribbean storm in characteristic style: she reared and bucked fearsomely, and what she couldn't get over she went through. She was taking green water up to the wheelhouse windows. Unlike the ordeal in the north Atlantic, the cook's leg remained intact, but the contents of his galley lay knee-deep on the deck. Yet Jake slept through it all. He had come a long way.

By the time they entered Curaçao harbour two days later the storm had passed and the ship's crew was slowly coming back to life. The exhausting effort of hanging on day and night to avoid being thrown on the deck or against a bulkhead was over. The desperately seasick began to eat a little food. And they were met with encouraging news: the last two tankers had had their propellers removed and were ready to go. Everybody headed for the nearest bar to celebrate. As a consequence, by the time they left with the *Chepita* and the *Carlota* in tow most of crew were again "more or less dead."

Under sunny skies they pulled their two charges toward Colón at speeds varying from 7 knots to 2. By the early morning of July 27 they were approaching the Canal Zone. Glancing astern to check the tow, John McQuarrie was startled to see a fleet of good-sized vessels overtaking him. Heedless of the tow, they foamed ahead, bones in their teeth, and threatened to become entangled in the towlines. John yelled warnings at them over the radio and, when they ignored him, swore at them—all to no avail. Only Norman Turner knew what was going on. He had gone ahead to the eastern end of the Canal to see his charges head through, stationing himself at a club on the very edge of the entrance. Another interested observer there was Aristotle Onassis, whose whaling fleet had been embargoed by Peru. The embargo had just been lifted, and Onassis told all and sundry that he had promised $10,000 to the first captain to get through the Panama Canal. A tow has highest priority in the canal zone and thus a ship towing several vessels has the unassailable right to be first in line. Ignoring this protocol the whalers charged past, endangering the tow, and raced into the Canal. Money talks.

Later that morning, the *Sudbury* handed the tankers over to the Panamanian crew who would see them safely through the canal, and by noon it was her turn to navigate the canal. The mess room was filled to bursting with their own crew and the Panamanians As they had done on the inward voyage, Ray and the cook were working frantically to keep up with this extra influx. However their guests were more than thoughtful: they insisted on doing all their own dishes and left the galley immaculate. Ray, increasingly disenchanted with the never-ending dishwashing, was more than grateful.

The Island Sovereign *arriving in Panama City.* Ray Sundby photo

By August 1 they were back on the west coast. Their insurers had decided that there must be two tugs for a tow this long so for ten days they waited there for the *Island Sovereign* to join them. Alf Armitage spent his free time on a do-it-yourself sightseeing tour. For 5 cents he rode each local bus to the end of the line and got a good look at Panama City. The only crew members who didn't go ashore were Hans Westergaard and Oscar Hodne. Having seen as much of the world as they wanted to, they gave Alf some money for a couple of bottles of Aquavit and stayed on board.

Before they left Curaçao, the tankers had been prepared for the open ocean: they had been checked for water, their anchors had been secured, their doors and entryways had been sealed, their battery boxes secured and their pipes cemented up. When the *Sovereign* finally arrived all they had to do was rig up the two tows, which was easier said than done. It now became apparent that they had too many cooks—or rather captains. Three captains and Norman Turner, all of them used to exerting authority, now argued about the way the tow should be rigged. Even after they had reached some kind of a consensus there was further acrimony. In his notebook Norman Turner noted wearily, "John McQuarrie complained bitterly and insisted that his 2" pennant was too long and shortened it to 600' against my decision. However he is the master of the tug."

Eventually, with all concerned (more or less) satisfied, the two tugs pointed their black bows in the direction of Victoria. It would take them forty days to get there, the *Sudbury*'s skipper estimated, and he was convinced that the *Sovereign* would make it first. Diesel is much superior to steam, he avowed. But it was not quite as he envisioned it to be.

Regardless of who got there first, forty days seemed an interminable length of time to the crew for whom each day blurred seamlessly into the next. Day after day the thin blue line of Central America crawled by off their starboard bow, without even passing ships to break the monotony. The sun beat down, turning bunks into bake-ovens; the Chief complained that the mess boy hadn't cleaned the bathroom properly; the second engineer complained that certain crew members were using too much water; everyone complained because they were running out of bed linen; the engine's bearings were overheating again; and the cook had exhausted his secret stash of liquor and was in a permanently vile humour.

Their snail's-pace progress made one diversion possible, however. They put out fishing lines and within an hour they had caught four fish: three tuna and an odd creature they couldn't identify. Transformed by this success, they became fanatical sport fishermen, none more so than the captain. He fished from dawn to dark, every strike bringing him down from the wheelhouse like a shot, eager to play his fish. They didn't eat their catch, however. Instead each trophy was carefully cleaned, wrapped and frozen to take back to Victoria.

Alf Armitage had brought two guns along: a .22 and a 300 Savage. Firearms are, as a rule, forbidden aboard ship but John McQuarrie chose to overlook this fact. To relieve their boredom, Alf and some of the others took potshots at tin cans and passing sharks and the crew became used to the sound of sporadic gunfire. One afternoon McQarrie and Alan Gray decided they were tired of popping at things with the .22 and got out the Savage. With her virtually noiseless steam engine the *Sudbury* was moving along serenely when, suddenly, several blasts from this rifle stopped all but the Chief dead in their tracks. This gentleman burst out of the engine room expecting a full-fledged mutiny at the very least. When he discovered the source of his fright "he was just wild."

Eleven days after their departure from Balboa, the *Sudbury* was off the coast of Mexico. Scanning the shore with binoculars as they reached Manzanillo, the crew saw a beautiful bay with a long white sand beach, a white cross on the hill above and an attractive town with a row of hotels fronting the ocean—the tropical paradise of their dreams. But viewing it through binoculars was as close as they would get to it. The *Sudbury* docked in Manzanillo to find that a Canadian destroyer was first in line to refuel and that they would have to wait till the next day to refuel. Despite the delay, their skipper gave them neither money nor permission to go ashore. Rounding them all up again from the bars that stretched down the beach would take more time than he was willing to spare.

By 10:00 a.m. on August 14 they had refuelled and were ready to leave, only to discover that the captain's fears had materialized. The cook and another crew member, Moose, were missing. The *Sudbury* blasted her whistle several times to no avail. Finally the immigration people came on board, got identification papers, fished the offenders out of a bar and presented them to their captain.

John McQuarrie didn't bluster and shout when he was angry and he rarely swore, but there was no mistaking his rage. He was doubly angry for he was angry at himself as well. He was the one who had recommended the cook for the job and he had spent the whole trip regretting it.

"I told you nobody goes ashore," he said through clenched teeth. "I've been blowing the whistle—"

"*I* didn't hear it, did you, Jimmy?" Moose asked the cook.

Jimmy thought it wiser to distract his captain, so he took another tack. Focussing a glassy stare in John's direction and affecting a winning smile, he said, "You should have come with us. We had a really, really good time."

"You've delayed us three hours," snarled John.

"We had a really—"

"Shut up," said his captain.

Assuming an air of aggrieved innocence, Jimmy tottered off to his cabin and fell heavily onto his bunk. When Ray Sundby tried to rouse him later to start dinner he was not in a co-operative mood. "You go to hell and take the dinner with you," he said. Ray relayed this message to the crew and they all came into the galley and made a horrible mess but they managed to get something to eat. They helped him clean up the mess, too, but they were a discouraged lot. Not only had dinner been a catch-as-catch-can affair, but word had got round that in Manzanillo one could buy 125 bottles of beer for $10.

For the next two days the captain pounded on the cook's locked door. "Go away," said the occupant. So Alan Gray put on an apron and took over. Having Ray and Alan in his galley slicing bacon made the cook so furious he decided that the captain had been unfair and that he would go on strike. Since he was already, in point of fact, not working, this threat failed to impress

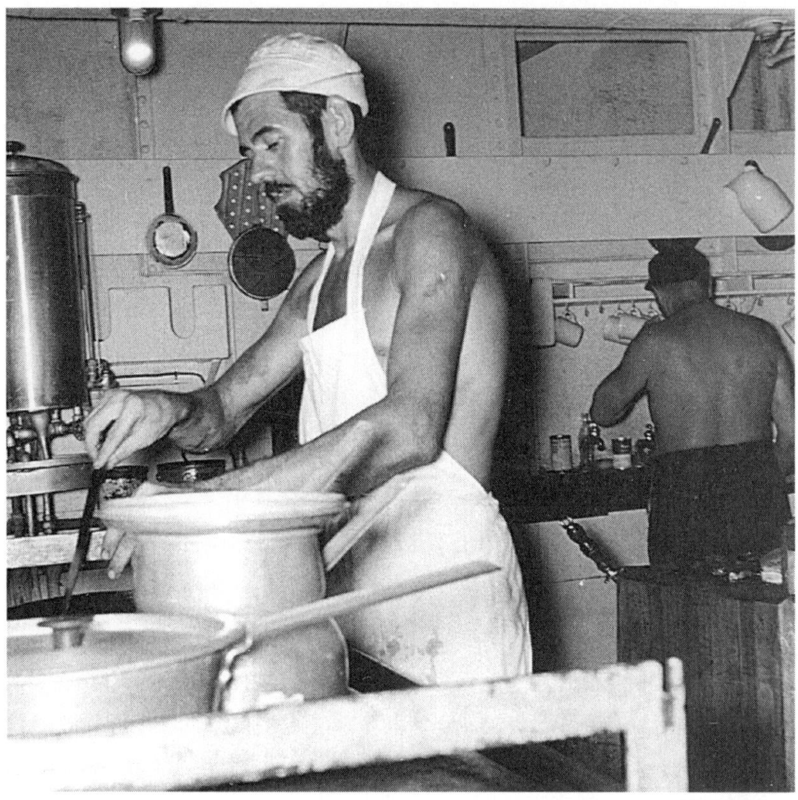

When the Sudbury*'s cook was indisposed, Alan Gray, the second mate, put on an apron and took over the galley.* Ray Sundby photo

the crew. Ray, who came from a sober Norwegian family, made up his mind about one thing. I'm never going to be a cook, he told himself. Imagine if I should end up like this guy.

The tow was now beset by mechanical problems besides culinary ones. Three hundred miles behind them the *Sovereign* had broken down. The *Sudbury* left her tankers anchored at Manzanillo and went to her rescue, towing both the *Sovereign* and her tow back to Manzanillo for temporary repairs. The *Sovereign* limped on to Los Angeles and the *Sudbury*, with all four tankers behind her, headed northward. "Did somebody say something about the superiority of diesel?" crowed her crew. "Nobody out-tows the *Suds*."

They were making 5 knots and for a mile astern the line of tankers stretched off to the horizon, a sight that astonished the crews of American tugs they encountered. "Oh my God, what the hell is that coming?" crackled one radio to another. "Looks like a train." And, as they got closer, "Would you believe it—it's a tug towing four big tankers!"

In the Caribbean the temperature in the engine room had reached 125°F and in the stokehold it was 148°. Off the coast of California, Ray Sundby's cabin was down to 82°, which he had come to think of as cool. The drop in temperature came too late for the food in the cooler, however. The heat of the past weeks had rotted most of its contents and the cook, on his feet again and dripping sweat into the food, threw all their bread and four cases of eggs overboard. Running short of everything, they ate pancakes and tried to eat the remaining eggs, without success. The eggs were either yellow or green, said Ray, and looked "rather mildewed." They threw another six cases into the sea.

In Panama City, those on the *Sudbury* had picked up a species of small beetle with a vicious bite. Now some of them reported having lice as well. There was much itching and scratching and the bosun became quite hysterical about the whole thing. Ray Sundby had other worries as well. He had a severe pain in his right side. He lay down whenever possible and hoped fervently that it wasn't his appendix. It was always so hot in his cabin that it was difficult for him to tell if he had a fever or not.

By the time they reached San Pedro the *Sovereign* had rejoined them. Each tug, in turn, went into the harbour for fuel, water and supplies while the other held onto the tow. The *Sovereign* went in first. Out in the Pacific, the *Sudbury* was soon enveloped in fog. Alf Armitage, standing at the rail staring into the thick grey blanket that surrounded them, was suddenly startled by the sight of a sleek little sport fishing boat that appeared not 10 feet away from where he stood. It came right up alongside the slow-moving tug and one of its occupants yelled, "Which way is true north?"

Alf, an engineer, had no idea. He called up to the bridge. "Which way is true north?" he asked Alan Gray.

"Why do you want to know?"

"There's a guy here who's lost."

Alan came down. "True north is 20 degrees that way," he said. "Where are you heading?"

"Actually we're heading for Catalina Island," said the intrepid sailors.

"Well, you're 20 miles south of Catalina Island and you're heading straight for China," was the reply.

This evidence of their incompetence was embarrassing enough, but worse was to follow.

"Could we buy 10 gallons of gas? We're just about out."

Alan woke John McQuarrie. "Nope," said John. "Won't sell you any gas."

Their faces fell.

"But I'll *give* you some. Have you got a compass? No? I thought not. Well I'll give you a compass, too, and then you follow the course I give you which will take you back where you came from. I think you better just forget about Catalina Island."

The *Sovereign* returned and now it was the *Sudbury*'s turn to go in for supplies. Visions of fresh fruit and vegetables danced before everyone's eyes and Ray took some comfort from the thought that civilization was at hand should he take a turn for the worse. As it turned out, this was not an idle thought. A doctor came aboard when they docked and promptly sent Ray off to the hospital for treatment of a serious infection. His crewmate, Moose, searching for a way to get off the ship, seized this opportunity to fake an appendix attack. His "symptoms" failed to impress the doctor, however. Ray was given a shot of penicillin and was sent back to the ship with a further supply, some needles and a syringe. Moose came right back with him.

The doctor had instructed Ray to lie in his bunk with his foot, swathed in a wet sheet, propped up on two pillows. The captain eyed this arrangement with suspicion. Illness was something John McQuarrie found difficult to understand, initially suspecting an element of malingering in this bedridden crew member, and he insisted Ray carry on with his duties in the galley. It was the cook who proved Ray's champion. "That kid is sick," he told the skipper. "He's got blood poisoning. That kind of thing can kill you." Even coming from such an unlikely source, this information hit home. The skipper reversed his decision and sent Ray back to bed. And as the days wore on he became his most solicitous attendant.

While Ray was off getting medical attention, John McQuarrie took the opportunity to have a radio technician come on board to solve some radio problems the *Sudbury* had been having. This man serviced the equipment and then tested it. While docked in San Pedro, *Sudbury* talked to Victoria on the radio-telephone and just about blew the local sheriffs out of their cars. Presently these gentlemen tracked down the source of the transmission and screeched up to the wharf, all armour and bluster, only to find a ship with a worldwide maritime licence for the same channel as their local one.

In the early evening of August 29 the *Sudbury* left San Pedro and found the *Sovereign* just where she had left her. Now both tugs and their tows settled in for the last lap of their journey.

Jack Daly was filling in for Ray Sundby as mess boy. A more unlikely mess boy could not have been found. Jack was a huge, raw-boned man who earned his living in the macho profession of deep-sea diving, and at first he was anything but happy about the menial job that had been thrust upon him. He warmed to the task, however, and was soon serving meals, washing dishes and even doing light laundry as if domestic science were second nature to him.

And the cook had a new role as well. In 1954 penicillin wasn't available in pill form, so each day Ray had to have an injection. The skipper had elected Jack mess boy; now he decreed that Jimmy be the one to administer the penicillin. If Jack was an unlikely domestic, Jimmy was an even more unlikely medical practitioner, but he approached the job in a businesslike fashion. First he took out the first-aid book, read the instructions and studied the illustration of a man's behind. There were lines drawn upon the picture to help the unskilled identify the proper place to insert the needle. "I've never done this before, you know," he said, consulting the book and fumbling with the syringe. This wasn't news to Ray. If he hadn't felt so acutely ill he might have fled. But the cook, having mastered the instructions and the intricacies of a syringe, appeared imbued with confidence. "Drop your pants," he ordered with authority.

He disinfected the injection site with a splash of whiskey and poured a shot for Ray. Then he himself downed a considerably larger drink. "Take aim. Fire!" he cried. He plunged the needle into Ray's posterior—or tried to. His calculations can't have been entirely accurate, however, for the needle delivered a painful jab and then bent.

"I'll put in a new needle and try a different angle," Jimmy said with all the confidence of vast experience.

This time it worked. Thank God that's over, thought Ray, struggling back to his bunk. He lay there, his leg in fearful pain, and thought with despair of the daily injections that lay ahead. Practice makes perfect, however—or something that approximates perfect. The cook delivered the subsequent injections with professional aplomb, each one of them preceded by a small shot of whiskey for Ray and a big one for himself.

Wind had now replaced the fog. "It was blowing like you wouldn't believe," said Alf Armitage. "The waves were huge. We were making less than 1 knot and the *Sovereign* was having a terrible time."

Behind them the tankers were barely visible. But Norman Turner's calculations proved equal to the weather and the towing gear held. By the time they reached Coos Bay the wind had dropped. In an effort to make better time they changed the towing gear to a tandem arrangement with the towlines forming a large *Y*. The wind changed direction as well; a following sea began to push them along at a respectable 6 or 7 knots. But even this improvement wasn't enough to quell the restlessness that everyone felt. They had been at sea for three months, their clean linen supply had run out, they were tired of each other and of the rusty hulks that trailed behind them and they wanted just one thing—to get home. The married men were anxious to see their wives and children and the unmarried were dreaming of an unlimited supply of beer.

Finally, on September 8, they heard the foghorn at the entrance to the Strait of Juan de Fuca. When the fog cleared they could see Vancouver Island. A plane from Canada Newsreel circled them several times taking pictures, and when they were still a couple of hours out of Victoria, the *Island Commander*, loaded with newspapermen, came out to meet them.

A mile-long tow had never been attempted before and the

naysayers said it couldn't be done. Now that it had been completed successfully and the naysayers were proved wrong, Harold Elworthy wanted this feat to receive the recognition it deserved and shed some glory on Island Tug & Barge in the process. Throughout the voyage he had kept the press informed of the ships' progress. Now, always clever at promoting his company, he hit upon a brilliant idea. Rather than wait for the press to come to the docks to interview the crew and take pictures, he decided to round up the media and *take* them en masse to the two ships. The offer of a free trip out into the Strait of Juan de Fuca on Island Tug's *Island Commander* proved an irresistible invitation, to say nothing of the fact that any who declined would be scooped by those who went. The tow got front-page coverage.

It was evening before the two ships anchored the tow by the Quarantine Station inside Race Rocks and entered Victoria Harbour. The Johnson Bridge went up, the *Sudbury*'s telegraph clanged, water churned out astern and she sidled into her moorage. Customs men were waiting to give the crew clearance to go ashore.

Next day Ray Sundby made the last entry in his diary: "September 9, 1954—Back to the tugboat. Worked till lunch and then we all signed off. Thank God. No more dishes; no more Jimmy; no more cabins to clean."

The *Victoria Daily Colonist*'s headline read: "4,000 Mile Towing Job Once Said Impossible" and there was even a diagram of the towing gear. The reporter, completely carried away by the romance of it all, painted a picture of a carefree jaunt to the tropics, the crew sleeping on deck in hammocks and shopping for souvenirs in each port of call. Had he cared to inquire, the *Sudbury*'s mess boy could have supplied him with a more accurate account of the voyage.

The Sudbury *and the* Island Sovereign *with their tow of four tankers. By the end of the voyage they had got it all together.* Bill Halkett photo, Seaspan

CHAPTER IV

The *Makedonia*

"Harley took the Sudbury *out and brought back the Greek— and the rest is history."*

For a year the *Sudbury* towed log barges down the BC coast, some of them converted from those same tankers she had brought up from South America. Pete Van de Putte remembers one of those trips. "We were in Queen Charlotte Sound in heavy weather. The barge was taking on water.

'Do you think we can save her?'

'Well, if she doesn't roll over.'

'And if the pump starts…'

"An oiler and I undertook to go back to the barge in the motor-boat; it took skillful boat-handling to get alongside the barge in the sea that was running and it took a lot of stupidity to attempt to get aboard that thing. It took an equal amount of stupidity to go down in the barge's engine room because she was listing 40 degrees by this time and at 55 they turtle. The pump started. We pumped away for thirty-two hours with no food and no heat."

And then, on the last day of October 1955, the master of the 8,200-ton freighter SS *Makedonia*, then 3,000 miles out in the north Pacific, sent the following cable to Lloyd's of London, via New York. English was not the captain's first language.

> At 5:00 am ship's time happen tremendous shake on engine and stop for 10 minutes then revolve engine dead slow to ascertain what happens. Had shakes on engine and hard noises on shaft at intervals. When daylight ascertain that propeller and nut are on but slack and shaft is not broken. Am disabled.

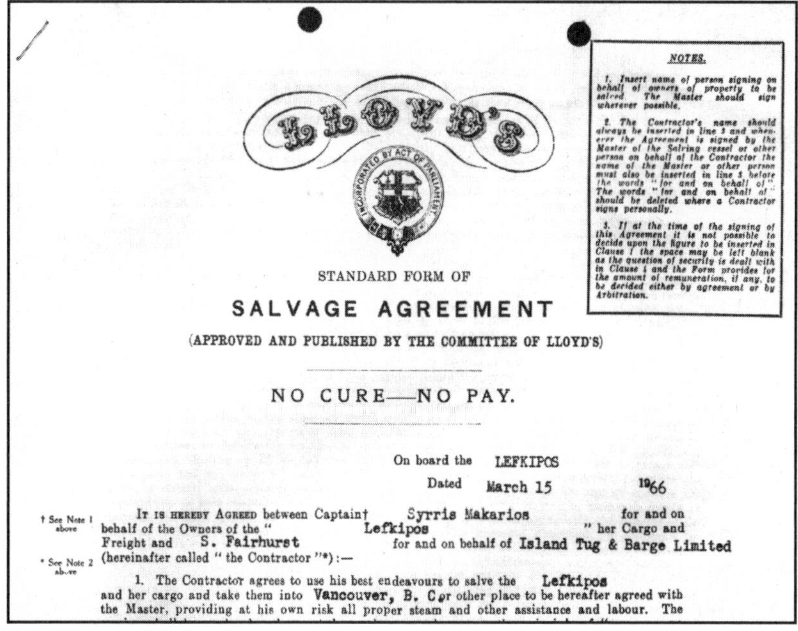

LLOYD'S

INCORPORATED BY ACT OF PARLIAMENT

NOTES.

1. Insert name of person signing on behalf of owners of property to be saved. The Master should sign wherever possible.

2. The Contractor's name should always be inserted in line 3 and whenever the Agreement is signed by the Master of the Salving vessel or other person on behalf of the Contractor the name of the Master or other person must also be inserted in line 3 before the words "for and on behalf of". The words "for and on behalf of" should be deleted where a Contractor signs personally.

3. If at the time of the signing of this Agreement it is not possible to decide upon the figure to be inserted in Clause 1 the space may be left blank as the question of security is dealt with in Clause 4 and the Form provides for the amount of remuneration, if any, to be decided either by agreement or by Arbitration.

STANDARD FORM OF

SALVAGE AGREEMENT

(APPROVED AND PUBLISHED BY THE COMMITTEE OF LLOYD'S)

NO CURE—NO PAY.

On board the LEFKIPOS

Dated March 15 1966

† See Note 1 above — IT IS HEREBY AGREED between Captain† Syrris Makarios for and on behalf of the Owners of the " Lefkipos " her Cargo and Freight and S. Fairhurst for and on behalf of Island Tug & Barge Limited (hereinafter called " the Contractor "*):—

* See Note 2 above

1. The Contractor agrees to use his best endeavours to salve the Lefkipos and her cargo and take them into Vancouver, B. C or other place to be hereafter agreed with the Master, providing at his own risk all proper steam and other assistance and labour. The

Lloyd's Open Form Salvage Agreement: "No Cure—No Pay." Seaspan

The only tug on the Pacific coast with a cruising range that permitted the rescue of the *Makedonia* was the *Sudbury*, so that same day the Freighters and Tankers Agency contacted Island Tug & Barge with the request that their big tug go to the *Makedonia*'s assistance. It was the opportunity Harold Elworthy and his ship had been waiting for.

At this point it was perhaps only H.B. who understood exactly what Island Tug stood to gain or lose by accepting this first offshore salvage job. Salvage is an unforgiving business and salvage laws, like most laws, are written in a language that resembles English. They bristle with sections and subsections; boiled down to the basics, they state that no salvor can attempt to salvage a ship without her master's consent. If consent is forthcoming, the ship's agent and the salvage company come to an agreement on the method of compensation: payment on an hourly basis, or on Lloyd's Open Form (LOF). The former option is as straightforward as it sounds: the salvor will exert every effort to save the vessel and will be paid for this effort by the hour. The latter states that the salvor will be paid if and when the rescue is successfully completed—or, as the bold black letters at the top of the LOF state, "No Cure—No Pay."

As a blank document the LOF has all the charm of a mortgage agreement; only a lawyer might find its three pages of clauses interesting reading. But a completed LOF tells a compelling story. Each of the seventeen or so words inserted in its blanks transforms it into a record of high drama and makes it clear that a crisis exists. By signing this document, the captain of the stricken ship—to his anguish, and that of the ship's owners—acknowledges that he is in desperate need of help. The captain of the salvage vessel has probably had a hair-raising experience just reaching the quarry. Now, by signing the same document, he agrees that he will put forth every effort to save her.

If the salvage is successful, a large salvage reward will be paid, the size dependent on the risks involved, the value of the ship and the value of her cargo. Thus, before a salvage vessel is dispatched, her owners must first gauge their chance of succeeding—and gauge it accurately, because it's not simply a matter of going out and doing your damnedest. No matter how valiant the efforts of the salvage vessel and her crew, if their quarry is not rescued and brought safely into port, they are paid nothing, not even their costs. Taking on the job of rescuing the *Makedonia* put both Island Tug's financial health and its reputation at risk. But H.B. had confidence in his ship and her crew and he was, by nature, a gambler. There was no hesitation on his part: the radio-telephones burst forth with a series of orders. The *Sudbury* dropped her tow in Andy's Bay and raced for Prince Rupert.

The *Sudbury*'s crew were told only that they were going to

Prince Rupert—nothing more. The youngest member of the crew was Eddie Gait. Brought up on a little hardscrabble farm in Saanich, he was fifteen when his parents decided they could no longer afford the luxury of sending him to school. He went to Victoria to look for a job and, since Island Tug was one of Victoria's largest employers, he haunted their premises until Fred Skinner finally hired him.

"Are you sure you're eighteen?" the man inquired, and Eddie solemnly assured him that he was.

On the farm this earnest, soft-spoken kid had learned to work hard. He soon graduated from the tiresome task of cleaning cylinder rings to a job on the *Challenger*, and it was there that Fred Skinner searched him out one day.

"Got another job for you," said Skinner. "*Sudbury* needs an oiler. How soon can you get your stuff?"

Eddie's "stuff" was in fact not much more than the clothes he stood up in. But at Mr. Skinner's insistence he took the bus home, gathered up a few things and headed back to the Island Tug dock.

On the *Sudbury*, Eddie found a surrogate family—and it started with his clothes. The engine room's iron gratings soon chewed up his only pair of shoes and one of the engineers, Dick Wade, resoled them with gasket material. He repeated this process three times before they returned home. And then there was the matter of his shirt.

As the days wore on, Ed's one shirt wore out. One day he was taken aside by the skipper, Steve Fairhurst. "Kid, I want to talk to you," he growled, making sure that no one else was within earshot. He then produced a paper bag containing a shirt and, without another word, turned on his heel and headed back to the wheelhouse.

Under Steve's tough-guy exterior was not only a heart of gold but a sense of humour. In port one day Eddie arrived in the crew's mess room to find every seat taken.

"Come and sit on our side," said Captain Fairhurst.

Eddie hesitated.

"Sit right down here next to me," said his skipper.

No sooner had Eddie reluctantly complied than the Chief

Engineer appeared. "He was deaf and he was a miserable bugger," remembers Eddie.

"Get out of my chair, kid," bellowed this individual.

"Don't you move," said Steve Fairhurst. "You sit right there."

Steak was served. To Steve Fairhurst's vast amusement, Eddie fumbled nervously with his knife and fork and his steak shot across the table, spraying gravy all over the Chief's shirt.

Glyn Holme recalls the only time he saw Steve bested in the mess room. "In the summer there were students working as deckhands. Every day for three weeks one of these kids said, 'Give me six pancakes.' Finally Steve couldn't stand it. 'The next bugger that asks for six pancakes, I'm going to fire.' 'I'll have five pancakes,' says the kid."

Among Eddie's special friends in the crew was Pete Van de Putte, the *Sudbury*'s third engineer. A broad-shouldered six-foot-six, Pete would become, in time, a great slab of a man. At twenty-three he was simply an immensely tall kid with a cowlick and a lop-sided grin; his oiler, Oscar Hodne, had promptly dubbed him Skeezix after a look-alike comic strip character. But there the similarity ended, for Pete had attended the college of hard knocks and was an unusually mature twenty-three-year-old. He was married, was about to become a father and, like a father—or perhaps a big brother—he took Eddie under his wing. One of the responsibilities he undertook was the task of augmenting Eddie's meagre education. During the long, tedious days that are part of life on a towboat, this unlikely pair sat down and tackled geometry, algebra and mechanics. Theoretically Eddie had completed grade eight, but since he was pulled out of school every time he was needed on the farm, which was frequently, his grasp of these things was tenuous at best.

"In those few months at sea I learned more than I had in five years of school," he said. Perhaps the most important thing he learned from Pete had nothing to do with academic subjects: "Just remember one thing, Eddie; if you ever expect to get anywhere at all in this world, you have to be a self-starter." Eddie knew that Pete himself was a self-starter, and he had enormous respect for him. He followed his advice from that moment on.

With the mate, Jimmy Talbott, Eddie staged wrestling matches and with John Hall, the cook, he had long heart-to-heart talks. If it hadn't been for occasional bouts of seasickness, things couldn't have been better for the farm boy from Saanich. Now he was heading for Prince Rupert and beyond on a great adventure.

By 7:00 a.m. on November 1, the *Sudbury* was in Prince Rupert harbour. Radio-telephone messages had preceded her and, immediately after her arrival, a convoy of trucks trundled down onto the dock. The tug's winch hissed steam, her boom swung toward the dock and sacks of flour, cases of vegetables, quarters of beef swathed in cheesecloth, boxes of chickens and butter and every other comestible required to feed sixteen men for an unknown length of time were lowered over the side on pallets and landed on the *Sudbury*'s deck. Island Tug crews had always complained loudly when forced to drink canned milk. Now cartons and cartons of fresh milk appeared on the pile of provisions. While the cook supervised the stowage of this mountain of food, the *Sudbury* moved to the oil dock and began to bunker fuel. Long-distance arrangements had been made to sign on two extra crew members, who arrived at the dock and climbed aboard: a mess boy who took to his bunk at the first big roll and didn't leave it for the remainder of the voyage, and a deckhand nicknamed "the Card Player." Suffice to say that neither was of Island Tug calibre. The *Sudbury*'s captain, John McQuarrie, was overdue for shore leave so Harley Blagborne, one of the few Island Tug masters with a deep-sea ticket, was tapped to take his place. At the time he was called, Harley's tug was crawling through Active Pass with a tow. He was plucked from her deck by a passing fish boat and flown to Prince Rupert. He arrived in the late morning, wended his way through the packing cases of food, conferred with the Chief, Walter Hitchen-Smith, and went up to the wheelhouse. By 2:00 p.m. the *Sudbury* was on her way—and the rest is history. For Harley Blagborne, the short, fair-haired man with the incandescent smile, and his ship, the *Sudbury*, would come to epitomize salvage on the coast of British Columbia.

Harley was reserved, conscientious to a fault and "very much a married man." He was born on a farm out of sight of the sea, yet grew to be an outstanding seaman. Now he was to meet another: the indomitable Christos Papaliolios, captain of the *Makedonia*.

Captain Papaliolios's troubles had begun the preceding January when his propeller shaft broke and he was towed into San Juan, Puerto Rico, for repairs. For some inexplicable reason, when the shaft was repaired the propeller was replaced with the *Makedonia*'s spare prop, a cast-iron one. Cast-iron propellers are meant for emergency use only. After extensive use, this one acted predictably: it worked loose and chewed the shaft. The resulting vibration threatened to tear the engine apart so it was shut down and the *Makedonia* wallowed silent and helpless. Christos Papaliolios was a man not easily beaten, however, and what he did next was astonishing. Among his crew members was a seaman who had served under sail. Under this man's supervision the deck crew took the tarpaulin off one of the hatches and cut it into two triangles. They then rigged these makeshift sails onto the *Makedonia*'s masts and booms, and this unwieldy craft sailed eastward for almost 300 miles. Still far from land, with a dwindling supply of food and water and the threat of bad weather, Captain Papaliolios finally threw in the towel and called for help.

Now, as the *Sudbury* beat her way out to the Greek, those in the pilothouse consulted charts for a bleak and unfamiliar string of islands: the Aleutians. There, at the top of the world, they rose suddenly out of the sea, shrouded in cloud, battered by storms, largely uninhabited. For these men, so familiar with every convolution of the BC coastline, this was a strange new territory with strange new names—Unimak Pass, Adak, Constantine Harbour, Sanak.

The weather that surrounds the Aleutian Islands is the worst in the hemisphere. During winter, storm follows storm in unending succession, the wind howling out of the north at 50–60 knots, bringing with it driving sleet and snow. The *Sudbury* was now proceeding on a course that would take her directly into this inhospitable area of the north Pacific. She had left Prince Rupert in fair weather but in a matter of days a series of gales generated by the Aleutian low bore down upon them. In the wheelhouse the telegraph rang from Full Ahead to Slow Ahead and the engine room reduced speed accordingly, but even at reduced

speed, waves swept over the *Sudbury*. Gigantic mountains of water rose up and then crashed down on her, smashing the gangplanks lashed on deck and pouring into the galley skylight. For hours on end they were forced to heave to. "I didn't know a lot about the sea," said Eddie Gait, "but it was hard for me to believe that the *Sudbury* could

The Sudbury *batters her way northward through mountainous seas in the Gulf of Alaska, 1955.*
Pete Van de Putte photos

take a beating like that and not break up."

In the engine room Pete Van de Putte and the rest of the black gang were largely unaware of what was going on above them, nor were they particularly interested. Their job was to keep the plant going and that task kept them fully occupied. Pete and Herb Marian, the second engineer, had discovered that they possessed complementary talents: Herb had the technical knowledge and Pete the dexterity with tools. "Between the two of us," Pete said, "we made one good engineer." Now they struggled with the air pump which gave them constant problems because the shuttle stuck. Pete, never one for subtlety, found that giving it a good blow was the answer. Periodically a shower of salt water coming down a ventilator reminded them that all hell was breaking loose on deck, and eventually the amount of water they were taking down the ventilator could no longer be ignored. The engine room gang drew straws and Eddie lost. It fell to this youngest member of the group to go up on deck and close the offending ventilator. For the first time since the trip began, Eddie was "scared stiff." Nonetheless he headed up the companionways to the top deck and then, for ten minutes, struggled to open the cabin door. Fighting against the wind and water that lashed at the other side of it, he finally got it open a few inches and began to squeeze through. He had one leg outside when the ship rolled onto her side and the heavy steel door came back on him. Desperate now, terrified that he would be crushed, he heaved against the metal with all his strength and managed to free himself. Now in the maelstrom outside, he crouched, clutching a rail. The ventilator was six feet away: to reach it—to relinquish his grip on the rail and transfer it to the ventilator—took all the willpower he could muster. As the ship rolled, he chose his moment and grabbed the ventilator with both hands. As he did so he discovered with dismay that his feet were no longer under him but straight out behind. He was attached to the ventilator as a flag is attached to a mast. Somehow he regained his feet, turned the ventilator and fought his way back inside the cabin. Back in the engine room, Pete asked, "What's the matter with your hands?"

Eddie looked down at his hands. Like an eagle's talons they were locked into a death grip.

"I knew it was going to be like that and I wish I'd lost the toss," said Pete.

The *Sudbury*'s radio operator was Percy Pike, a former lighthouse keeper. As the tug fought her way out into the north Pacific he kept in touch with the *Makedonia* and relayed her position to Harley. Each time he did, the *Sudbury* altered her course slightly in order to keep her as yet invisible quarry dead ahead. Recording a succession of latitudes and longitudes is not the most inspiring task and it loses what little charm it might have when the recorder is being thrown from one side of his cabin to the other. Percy had taken to sitting on the deck to dress, but even there it was a struggle to pull on his pants. But then, on November 7, monitoring the short-wave distress band, Percy heard a voice that erased his boredom and discomfort.

"This is Pavlof Harbour calling. To anyone who can hear this message. Please come in. I repeat. This is Pavlof Harbor calling. We have a medical emergency."

Ships avoid the Great Circle Route in the north Pacific in the winter. No other voice responded.

"This is Pavlof Harbor..." The voice was faint and desperate.

Percy turned on his transmitter.

"This is SS *Sudbury* to Pavlof Harbor. Can I be of assistance?"

Even through the static, Percy could hear relief in the other voice.

"To the SS *Sudbury*. We have a woman here who has just given birth. She's in great pain and she seems to be paralyzed. Can you get us some medical help?"

Percy changed channels and made contact with the US Coast Guard. A Coast Guard doctor's crisp voice emerged from the radio.

"It appears that you're the only one that can hear both sides of this conversation, *Sudbury*, so you'll have to relay my instructions to Pavlof Harbor. Ask them what drugs they have."

"We have administered penicillin; that's all we have here," came the answer via Percy.

"Bathe the patient in warm water," said the doctor. Which sounds a bit silly, Percy thought, as he relayed the message.

For twenty-four hours, while the woman's condition was

monitored and a plane dispatched, he sat glued to his radio set and this tense three-way conversation. Only when the patient was safely en route to Anchorage by plane did he remember the *Makedonia*.

Five days later, on November 12, the *Sudbury* finally reached the stricken ship. In that vast open ocean the dot that was the *Makedonia* appeared first on the radar screen and then on the horizon. "God, she looks lonely," said Harley to the helmsman. Lonely and battered. The wind had gone down, leaving an enormous groundswell rolling over the surface of the sea, and in the early winter darkness the *Makedonia*, in ballast, high in the water, lay there rolling with it. "When it's really windy the waves are 40 or 50 feet high," Eddie Gait explained. "But when a storm subsides, the wind isn't cutting the tops off the waves, so the waves were so high that the *Makedonia* would go out of sight—and that thing was 70 or 80 feet high."

Harley swung the *Sudbury*'s stern in a boat-length from the Greek. On the low afterdeck, the tug's deck crew craned their necks up at the wall of steel above them. On the crest of a swell the *Makedonia* stared right down the *Sudbury*'s funnel. And then the swells heaved the *Sudbury* into the air and dropped the *Makedonia* down into the trough. For moments the tug's crew were looking down on the freighter's decks. Jim Talbott, the tug's first mate, stood on the stern clutching the *Sudbury*'s rocket gun. As the tug rose up to meet the *Makedonia* he aimed, turned his face away from the upcoming blast and fired. The heaving line snaked across the water and over the freighter's bulwarks.

There was a scramble for it and the crewmen hauled it in. There was a heavier line to follow and then the towing wire to be connected, but it was the taking of that first light line that confirmed the Greek as salvage and the *Sudbury* as salvor. That heaving line, proffered by one ship and accepted by the other, committed the parties to the terms of the LOF.

Should the *Sudbury* be able to deliver her charge into Vancouver Harbour safely, Island Tug would reap a rich reward. Should she fail, the company would get nothing at all.

The towing wire was coupled up to the *Makedonia*'s anchor chain, 2,000 feet of wire was paid out and the tow began. But

The Sudbury*'s mate, Jimmy Talbott, fires the rocket gun toward the* Makedonia. Pete Van de Putte photo, Seaspan

when it did, the Greek captain got a nasty shock. As Pete Van de Putte said, "He must have just about turned himself inside out when he realized he was being towed to the west coast of Canada and not to Japan. Because he was damned near *in* Japan." The change in direction was H.B.'s decision. This was the *Sudbury*'s first offshore salvage job and Harold Elworthy, with his unerring instinct for publicity, knew that if she returned in triumph to her home port there would be front-page news coverage that would be picked up by the newspapers in every major seaport in the world.

And so they sailed toward the coast of British Columbia—right into another storm. Speed reduced to 3 knots, they struggled on. Harley felt that if the *Makedonia* could use her prop, even to a limited extent, it would help. On this principle the two ships made it into Adak Harbor. There, assisted by the US Navy, the *Makedonia*'s forward tanks were flooded so that her propeller was out of the water; then, working from a navy scow, the *Sudbury*'s engineers did their best to tighten the propeller onto the shaft. This pause gave the rest of the crew the welcome opportunity to go ashore and stretch their legs, and it provided Eddie with one of his more memorable moments in the voyage. Walking up the wharf he encountered rats as big as cats; 18 inches long, they confronted the strollers with open defiance.

The voyage continued into the worst weather they had yet experienced. The log reads "Overcast, rain, very heavy seas and swell." The "very heavy seas" were 40 feet high and the wind had reached 70 miles an hour. The *Makedonia* radioed that her propeller was loose again and that she had stopped her engines. She was yawing badly. On the *Sudbury* the crew clung to stanchions, fought for balance, braced themselves, even in sleep. Walter Hitchen-Smith, the Chief and Scottie Miller, one of the oilers, didn't even have the resilience of youth on their side. Both were in their sixties, but they were tough old birds who had somehow learned to sleep in such conditions—or to function without it. Oscar Hodne had his own line of action. Having had two ships sink under him, he had no intention of being caught in his skivvies. Each night he changed into a clean T-shirt and jeans and slept in these clothes.

They were all used to a ship working under a load. If that load was suddenly relieved they felt it, even in their sleep. Suddenly Pete Van de Putte was wide awake. He opened his cabin door and his question was answered before he asked it. "We've lost the Greek," somebody said.

It was 8:00 p.m. Almost immediately the *Makedonia*'s running lights disappeared into the blackness. The *Sudbury*'s log reads "Chain parted on deck of *Makedonia*." Instantly everyone on the tug applied himself to this new circumstance.

On the careening stern of the *Sudbury*, sometimes waist-deep in the waves that swept her, the deck crew hauled in their 2,000 feet of wire, dragging the 30-ton weight of the *Makedonia*'s anchor chain as they did. When the chain finally reached them they unshackled it and let it drop.

In the engine room Eddie's job, for two watches, was to engage and disengage the emergency steam valve. Freed from the restraining weight of the towline, the stern was pointing skyward each time the bow barrelled down into the trough. "A ship like the *Sudbury* was too small to ride out a 70- or 80-foot wave," Eddie explained, echoing the sentiments of the British Admiralty sixteen years before. "The prop comes out of the water and you have to have the steam shut off several seconds before it comes out. Otherwise the prop just goes crazy and when it hits the water again it will break something." And so he stood there hour after hour, and after a while his timing got pretty good.

In the wheelhouse, Harley peered into the blackness, noted the waves and waited for the right moment. It was a long time coming. Finally he saw his opportunity. "Hard aport," he said to the helmsman. "Make her swing." Freed from her restraining position heading into the seas, the *Sudbury* lunged wildly and then, broadside to the seas, she rolled so far over that it seemed she would capsize, but she righted herself. "Ease her up," said Harley. Now the seas were towering up behind her. Through the night the radar tracked the *Makedonia* and, having found her, the *Sudbury* "steamed slow, standing by." The weather made any other action impossible.

By noon on Friday, November 25, the weather had moderated to some degree. With both ships still rolling wildly the *Sudbury* prepared to try reconnecting with her tow. Her laconic log gives no indication of the seamanship that this required. "Towing gear o.k. Tow apparently o.k.," it says. "Moving into position to put line on the *Makedonia*. Line aboard at 14:45 after couple of unsuccessful attempts due to fresh to strong winds and heavy swell." Then, lest there be any misapprehension regarding the weather, it adds, "Overcast, rough confused seas, heavy swells." The swells were so heavy that the big merchantman disappeared from sight in their troughs.

The twenty-four hours during which the *Makedonia* was on her own were harrowing for the Greeks. Her bulk driven by the wind, the ship drifted for miles, working her way inexorably toward the rock-strewn shore—a shore invisible in the darkness, but clearly visible on the radar, and Captain Papaliolios knew that it was white with crashing waves. He made his decision. He had to have steerage. He must have power.

"No, no, no," protested his Chief. "If that propeller vibrates badly enough it will break a steam pipe and kill all of us in the engine room."

"Sometimes one is obliged to cut off his finger to save his life. If you don't obey my order *I* will kill you," was the reply.

The Makedonia *under tow in very heavy seas.* Pete Van de Putte photo

Slowly the *Makedonia*'s propeller began to revolve, convulsing the ship with its vibration. The vessel headed into the wind slowly and inched away from destruction. Captain Papaliolios's gamble had paid off. Once more coupled together, and with the storm still raging, the two ships fought their way back to the course for Kodiak, Alaska. They arrived there on December 1, in the first good weather they had had in weeks, and the *Sudbury* bunkered fuel. Even before they left, however, the weather had deteriorated once again and by the time they reached the Gulf of Alaska they were being battered by yet another raging gale. Harley radioed Victoria: "Winds Force 12. Hove to. Have made no headway in the last twenty-four hours."

Harold Elworthy had put cameras, both still and movie, aboard the *Sudbury*. Their pictures were to form part of the salvage report. Even today, even viewed from the security of a landlubber's sofa, these movies evoke stark terror. They dramatically illustrate the real meaning of that spare notation, "Very heavy seas." That anyone could keep his head, let alone proceed with a towing job, under those conditions is cause for amazement.

And yet they did. Harley, always quiet and contained, put aside the idea of sleeping. Pete Van de Putte, too young to know any better, kept struggling with the air pump. Jim Talbott, he of the rocket gun, nursed the bump the tow's anchor chain had delivered to his head. And Herb Marian was not only thrown around with all the rest, but, unknown to most, coping with epilepsy as well.

Harley Blagborne, the Sudbury*'s captain, being congratulated at Prince Rupert. Ed Gait is at left; Percy Pike, the radio operator, is at right.*
Jack Wrathall photo, Seaspan

Finally they approached Prince Rupert and the promise of more sheltered waters. They picked up two pilots off Triple Island. The Greek was behaving herself and the trip down the Inside Passage would be in waters calmer than any they had encountered since their departure.

The ship had been at sea for over five weeks. For most of that time—for twenty-four hours on most of those days—her crew had been slammed around on a ship that never stopped pitching and rolling. They were exhausted. George Matson, recounting a similar experience, found it difficult to put into words. "How do you explain it?" he said. "It's not nearly as bad as people imagine and yet it's far bloody worse. It's a paradoxical thing. For one thing it's absolutely miserable, if nothing else. Nobody sleeps. You can't eat properly. In my case I frequently got so seasick that I could barely stand. But you simply can't explain it. Day after day after day after day hanging on by your fingernails the whole time." So the *Sudbury*'s crew were counting the days until the end of this odyssey and looking forward to their richly deserved shore leave once the vessel touched the dock in Vancouver. The oilers were planning to head straight for their favourite beer parlour; Harley would be welcomed by his devoted wife, Ann; and Pete would be seeing his new daughter for the first time, for she was born while the *Sudbury* was away on this gruelling tow. With the end of the voyage in sight, Pete was considering how he would spend his bonus money. His plans were neither greedy nor grandiose: he decided that with a new baby, buying a refrigerator would be the best use for it.

Their ordeal was not yet entirely over, however. Harold Elworthy, PR man that he was, had no intention of allowing the successful completion of this 3,200-mile tow to go unnoticed. The newspapers were alerted and reporters and photographers from the Vancouver dailies set off hell-bent on the trail of the story. They arrived by sea and air and they jumped aboard from a hastily commandeered fish boat. They interviewed everyone from the captain to the cook and monopolized the radio-telephone to send their stories back to their papers. Despite his fatigue and his ongoing responsibilities Harley put up with all this with good grace, answering questions, posing for pictures and managing to remain co-operative and pleasant. But for some of the crew this intrusion proved to be the last straw. Off Howe Sound Pete came off watch and found his cabin occupied by a stranger.

"Name's Jack Webster," said the man, briskly, pencil at the ready. "I'm with the program 'City Mike'—"

"Get outta my face," said Pete, and shoved him out the door.

Homeward bound. Seaspan

The reporters, of course, were only trying to do their job and some of them were displaying remarkable resourcefulness in this regard. Norman Hacking's paper, the *Vancouver Province*, got wind of the fact that the *Vancouver Sun* was sending a reporter to intercept the *Sudbury*. Norman and Villy Svarre, the newspaper's photographer, were dispatched at once on a small plane to Prince Rupert. Fog prevented them from landing and they found themselves dumped, instead, in Terrace. It was a wintry December and the Skeena Highway was closed, as was the railway. Undeterred, Norman found a taxi owner, a woman who had just recently arrived from England, had only just started driving a taxi and had never even *been* to Prince Rupert. Nonetheless, the spirit that built the British Empire must have burned brightly in this woman's breast for she agreed to get them to Prince Rupert and off they went, tearing down the Skeena Highway. This intrepid lady was as good as her word but when they arrived at their destination, they discovered that the *Sudbury*, making a good 12 knots, had passed Prince Rupert and had entered Fitzhugh Sound. Once more they searched out an unconventional but willing entrepreneur. They found the owner of a small float plane that was normally used for local freighting and contracted with him to fly them out to find the *Sudbury*. Villy and his cameras occupied the one passenger seat that the plane offered, Norman stretched out on the floor behind and they set off to find their quarry—not an especially difficult task, since a big tug towing a towering freighter is not easily overlooked. But as they skimmed over the water, within spitting distance of the waves below, they realized that their frustrations were not over. There was absolutely no chance that the *Sudbury*, finally making good time, would stop or even slow down for uninvited guests. Not to be stymied at this stage the pair arranged to have the pilot drop them at the nearest community ahead of the ship, which happened to be Bella Bella. There they found a Native fish boat captain adventurous enough to take them on the last lap of their journey.

Because Norman Hacking had actually served on the *Sudbury* during the war, he was familiar with her layout and knew where they had the best chance of scrambling onto her deck. The Native

The Sudbury *towing the* Makedonia *in BC waters.* Seaspan

captain followed his instructions to the letter and with both boats travelling at full speed he came alongside and remained there for perhaps two minutes. Norman and Villy, with the camera equipment, made a flying leap onto the tug and the fish boat sheered away, her captain no doubt reflecting with puzzlement on the strange ways of the white man.

The two proceeded to the bridge and introduced themselves to a bemused Harley Blagborne.

"And where are the heroes?" demanded Villy, anxious to get on with the job.

"The only heroes on this ship are you two damn fools," said Harley.

As the *Sudbury* approached Vancouver there was much lively betting on the actual time the ship would pass under Lions Gate Bridge. Her crew spent all their spare moments measuring distances on a dog-eared road map and consulting with the deck officers. In the end it was Eddie Gait, "the kid," who won the pot. A day or two out of Vancouver they played their last card game. All through the voyage the deckhand they had picked up in Prince Rupert had lost in these games, or perhaps broken even. Now, in this final game, the Card Player took them all, winning "just about everything on the ship."

On Sunday, December 11 the *Sudbury* neared Vancouver Harbour. The reporters who had descended upon them earlier had told the crew that their arrival in Vancouver was expected, but that did not prepare them for the welcome awaiting them. "We were treated like heroes," said Eddie in wonderment. At Roberts Creek H.B. and a party of friends came out into the strait on board the *Sea Lion* and greeted the returning crew with a long song from her famous musical whistle. The *Sudbury* replied with one long businesslike blast and two short ones, a message both self-evident and triumphant—the fog signal "I have a tow."

The harbour itself had been cleared of shipping to enable the *Sudbury* to manoeuvre her charge without distraction, so there were no other whistles to greet them. But on the Lions Gate Bridge and all around Stanley Park car horns made up for this. Alerted to the *Sudbury*'s return by the previous evening's paper, drivers sounded their horns in a wild cacophony of sound. This was the publicity that would put Island Tug on the map. As Pete Van de Putte said, "H.B. couldn't have bought that front page for a million dollars. He got it all for free—and got paid besides."

The Victoria Chamber of Commerce later presented Harley Blagborne with a commendation, which read:

> This testimonial is presented to Captain William Harley Blagborne, Master of the Victoria-based salvage vessel *Sudbury* (892 Tons) on the occasion of the completion of the rescue of the SS *Makedonia* (8200 Tons) which was disabled in the North Pacific Ocean some 3200 miles from the Port of Vancouver, British Columbia.
>
> The courage, devotion to duty, and determination to succeed, by the entire crew of the *Sudbury* resulted in victory over the most vicious elements of the high seas and the safe return of the SS *Makedonia*'s thirty-three man crew.
>
> This wonderful feat began October 31, 1955 and ended December 11, 1955.

Such an accomplishment is a magnificent example of the practical application of that section of the Jaycee creed which reads:

"We believe that service to Humanity is the best work of Life."

December 21, 1955

But now, as the *Sudbury* approached the harbour, a small knot of people stood on the dock, stamping their feet in the December cold as they waited patiently. First they waited on one dock and then, when the *Sudbury*'s plans changed, they hurried to another. When she finally docked, Harley, freshly shaven and in his shore-going clothes, stepped ashore, followed by his crew. Harold Elworthy, his eldest son and his grandson were among those on the dock. Filled with excitement and pride, Harold's son sprang forward to shake Harley's hand but H.B. restrained him. "Don't you step into the limelight, Art," he said. "This moment of glory belongs to the crew." And so they stood and watched as flashbulbs popped and Harley sought out his tiny wife, Ann, and hugged her. A TV cameraman who had missed the gesture asked the Blagbornes to repeat their embrace for the camera. Harley, who had never done anything for effect in his life, wasn't about to start now. He refused the request. He was a private man and, for him, the voyage was over.

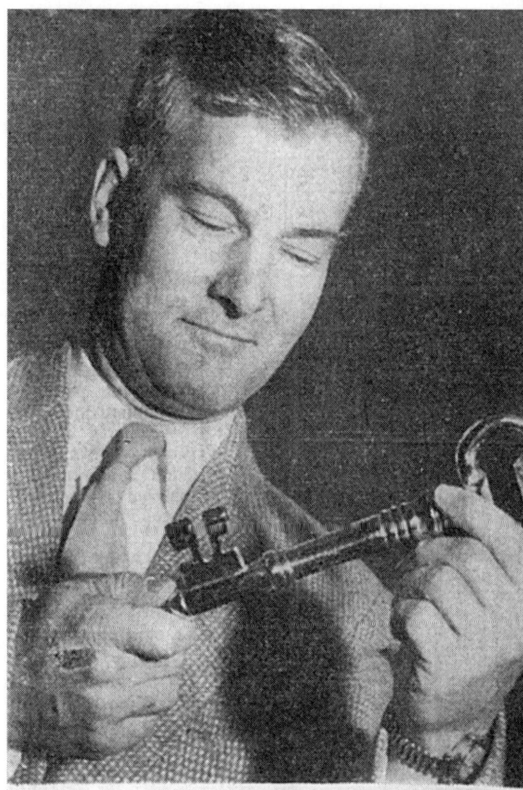

VICTORIA TUG HONORED

Captain Blagborne being presented the key to the city of Sudbury, Ontario sometime after the Makedonia *incident.*
Vancouver Maritime Museum

CHAPTER V

The *Straits Maru* et al

"When you start off on a journey like this, you don't realize until you're in the thick of it how much you depend on each other."

As a result of the *Makedonia*'s successful rescue, the *Sudbury* retained both her name and her captain. Harold Elworthy had intended to give her a new name with an "Island" prefix but now, almost overnight, the name *Sudbury* was known in maritime circles the world over, so it was too late for a name change. Indeed, as her exploits continued, the town of Sudbury, bursting with pride, presented her captain with the key to their city.

And Harley Blagborne's consummate seamanship had made Island Tug's name in salvage circles. In Harley, H.B. had found a man whose devotion to the company was absolute. George Hunter commented, "H.B. thought the world of Harley because Harley really produced for him. One day when Harley was off on the boat, his wife, Ann, had a question about Harley's pay. She went in and had an argument with some brash young guy in the office. He said, 'Now look, even a dumb woman can understand that.' Well, that got back to Harley, Harley got onto H.B. and that guy was sorted out in a hurry. Now that was a fairly commonplace comment for those days, but he picked the wrong person when he picked Harley's wife."

For Harley, his family and his job were his life. Originally a farm boy, he proved to have innate and outstanding skills as a mariner. Early in his career he had sailed on the five-masted topsail schooner *City of Alberni*. Perhaps it was on her that he absorbed his impressive knowledge of lines and rigging. George Hunter remembers him conferring with Harry Tebbs over a towline. Harley looked at a splice and said, "I don't like that." Neither of the others could see the slightest thing wrong with it, yet when it was checked the middle was found to be stranded. This sixth sense, this conscientious attention to detail, was ever present. At regular intervals Harley, personally, turned over all the portable pumps they carried to make sure they were in working order; he, personally, oversaw the scraping and painting done by Ray Thomas, a deckhand, to make sure it was up to yacht standard. It was a joke among the crews that he was "the highest paid bosun in the fleet." Yet when lives and property are at stake, a sense of personal responsibility can be a valuable commodity. Years later Harley's widow, Ann, said, "You know that big ferry that capsized and sank in the English Channel because the doors weren't secured? That would never have happened if Harley had been on board." No doubt she was right.

After the *Makedonia*'s rescue, the *Sudbury* became Harley's ship. In September of 1956, as she prepared for a trip to Japan with the barge *Straits Maru*, he was her captain. The *Straits Maru*, loaded with a cargo of scrap-car blocks, was the converted hull of an old Cunard liner and as a barge she left much to be desired. The *Sudbury*'s crew battened down the hatches and took their charge out off Esquimalt to see how it towed. Not well, it appeared: the *Straits Maru* wandered all over the place. They tried various solutions to the problem, with no success. They returned to Victoria to try again the next day. Three times Ray Thomas said goodbye to his family and for three days the *Sudbury*'s crew tried to remedy the situation. Nothing worked. Finally, on September 7, they gave up and took off with the *Straits Maru* yawing away behind them.

In the wheelhouse they plotted a course up and around the most northerly part of the Pacific Ocean. The *Sudbury* left first BC's coastline behind her and then Alaska's. Off the starboard bow glimpses of the Aleutian Islands appeared out of the overcast as they headed toward Unimak Pass. Soon the names of this distant and exotic string of islands would trip off the tongues of the *Sudbury*'s crew, and its harbours and passes would become as familiar to them as those of the BC coast. But on this first trip to Japan it was still unfamiliar territory.

They arrived at Unimak Pass on a beautiful flat calm Sunday—a pause amid the persistent Aleutian storms. By midnight the weather had become more typical: the tug and her tow were battling heavy seas and a howling gale. Throughout the night the mate's eyes seldom left the radar screen and the reassuring blip remained astern. At first light on Monday the anxious deck crew were able to check their tow visually. Through the flying spume they could see the *Straits Maru* lunging about at the end of the towline like a terrified animal. And worse, she was settling aft. Waves were breaking over her stern, and her bow was gradually coming out of the water and beginning to point skyward in that horrifying position that precedes a plunge to the depths, stern first.

Being pulled under by a sinking tow is a towboater's worst nightmare. Harley stationed a man at the winch's brake. Poised for the order "Let her go," the man stood ready to take off the brake and let the towline spin off the drum, which Harley hoped would break the shackle at its bitter end. Then Harley advised Victoria: "Very heavy weather. Tow taking on water. Attempting to reach Makushin Bay."

Harley hadn't envisioned a stop in the Aleutians and was happiest, in fact, well offshore. But now he was approaching a strange harbour with no large-scale charts and no other tugs close enough to assist. What's more, he was not even sure that his message to Victoria, relayed through Adak, had reached its destination. The *Sudbury*, with the *Straits Maru* wallowing behind her and a deckhand standing tensely by the winch brake, was very much alone.

In the shelter of the land the seas dropped and the straining tug gained the entrance of bleak and beautiful Makushin Bay. Harley issued quiet orders and the crew began to make their preparations. Most of the men were new to salvage work and many were new to each other, yet they worked together smoothly and efficiently. As Ray Thomas said, "When you start off on a journey like this you don't realize until you're in the thick of it just how much you depend on each other. You rely so much on the fact that the other fellow knows what he's doing. You're working together so much that you just operate as a team. You never had to tell anybody what to do—everybody knew. They just did it."

Now even as some of the crew were hauling in the towline, others were dragging the tug's portable pumps on deck. They were hardly alongside the waterlogged hulk before men were scrambling over the bulwarks, heaving the pumps with them. They were efficient, large-capacity pumps. Roaring into life, they stayed the water in the *Straits Maru*'s rusty hull, and then began to lower it. For a week the staccato sound of the pumps never stopped and water poured overboard in a steady stream. Then the salvors, down in the black depths of the hull, drove wooden plugs into holes and caulked around them with oakum. Next they built forms and poured concrete patches over the plugs. And then, having come within a hair's breadth of losing their tow, the voyage continued.

Ray Thomas had come from the British Merchant Service where he had trained as a cadet. That training included navigation. A lowly deckhand on his first voyage with Island Tug, Ray now had a chance to practise his navigating skills. Harley was, at this point, plagued by seasickness, and had never been enthusiastic about navigating. So Ray made his calculations, conferred with his captain and plotted a good part of the route to Japan.

Considering the state of their tow, those in the *Sudbury*'s pilothouse gave weather reports close attention and, nearing Japan, heard a report that lowered their spirits considerably. They had already noticed an ominous swell—long and slow, it rolled across the ocean, lifting the *Sudbury* gently and then dropping her—and the barometer, having jogged up and down for a day or two like a nervous stock market, was now falling steadily. So they weren't surprised to hear a hurricane warning broadcast on the marine band. The sea, it appeared, was going to make one last grab for the *Straits Maru*.

Typhoons change course and direction with maddening deviousness. The *Sudbury*'s captain, taking careful note of the storm's course and direction, did what he could to avoid it but the tail end of it caught the plodding *Sudbury*. With startling suddenness the storm erupted from the black sky and enveloped the tug. The seas, which had been a hissing angry grey, now became a solid churning white, as if beaten by some gigantic mixmaster. Astern, almost invisible in the flying scud, the *Straits Maru* hung on grimly. Hour after hour, lonely and desperate, she yawed away behind the tug.

For those on the *Sudbury* with deep-sea experience a typhoon was not a novelty—although towing in one was. For those whose experience had been limited to coastal waters this storm was an awe-inspiring education. "As an ignorant kid the whole thing just totally amazed me," said Eddie Gait. "It was a beautiful day—the sun was out—a really nice day. Within two to three minutes it was pitch black—it was totally black. The air was full of water; it was just a mass of water blowing. We were taking the wind on the port side of the ship and it battered hell out of us for hours. Then, all of a sudden, it was flat calm again. You could see daylight again. Then bango on the other side of the ship. I'd never realized what kind of a complete circle a storm is."

Miraculously the *Straits Maru*'s patches held. The *Sudbury*'s crew had kept this ancient hulk from sinking, had towed her halfway across the world and had shepherded her through a typhoon. Now in the harbour at Osaka they delivered her to her destination and anchored.

In the harbour there, small boats came alongside the *Sudbury* selling souvenirs. Ray Thomas, enjoying a respite from their arduous weeks, was in the mood for a joke. He decided to turn the tables on these super salesmen so with gestures he indicated to one boatman that he didn't want to buy but to sell. And what did he have to sell, the boatman indicated. Ray cast around him—the pennant, he would sell their pennant. He held one end of it up for inspection and he and the boatman began to haggle over price. Little did the boatman know that the portion he was looking at comprised part of 1,000 feet of wire, enough to sink his little boat. As the two bargained, Ray caught sight of Harley; without further ado he began pushing the pennant over the side toward the boat.

"What are you doing with that?" snapped Harley.

"I'm selling it to this guy."

"Like hell you are." Harley was not amused.

Life on the *Sudbury* was serious enough most of the time, Ray reflected glumly. You have to have *some* fun. But fun wasn't Harley's strong suit, and he was easily teased. John Henderson recalled his own joking with Harley: "We had been out in Japan in dry dock for a month and George Hunter and I had gone on a monumental bender. So one day when I was visiting on the *Sudbury II* I thought I'd have some fun with Harley. I said, 'I'm coming with you this trip as second engineer.'

'Oh?'

'George Hunter is coming as third mate.'

'Oh my God,' said Harley, 'I can't have that. I've got to go to the office and see about this right now. I don't mind one of you guys but not the two of you. Never again the two of you.'"

Harley's obsessive devotion to his job made him a superlative employee but a demanding superior and his expectations were sometimes unreasonably high. When his standards *were* met, however, he was quick to show his appreciation. Out in the Aleutians after the deck crew had laboured all day in waist-high seas and driving sleet, he invited them all up to his cabin. "Bring a mug," he said. He poured them all a hefty slug of rum. It was his wordless way of saying thank you.

So it was his exacting work ethic, not hard-heartedness, that nearly provoked a riot on this first landing in Japan. After five weeks at sea the crew of the *Sudbury* were desperate to get ashore, to get their mail, to get a break from each other. Perhaps their captain was afraid carousing would make them unfit for work the next day; perhaps he was simply incapable of understanding those who didn't share his workaholic nature. In any event, for whatever reason, Harley refused to give them any money. The enraged crew resorted to pounding on the locked door of their captain's cabin. Harley remained obdurate.

The tug spent three days in port loading provisions and bunkering fuel; then, free of her lumbering tow, she left on the return trip to Victoria, travelling at a good 13 knots.

The cook on this trip was neither Ray Sundby's nemesis, Jimmy, nor Eddie Gait's idolized John Hall. He was a big Greek, a former fireman who was inclined to wave a cleaver and shout, "Out of my galley!" at any kibitzers. This menacing manner, plus his size, intimidated the crew. No one dared complain about the food; instead when canvassed by him (as they often were) everyone praised his culinary prowess extravagantly. Eddie Gait, who had avowed, when thus closely questioned, that the cook's shortbread was "out of this world," found himself inundated with the stuff. It filled every crevice under his bunk and he was at pains to know what to do with it. And René Fournier had this to add: "The cook seemed to have trouble making decent hotcakes so the oilers on the third engineer's watch would dump the cook's batter each night and make up some more. At breakfast time the cook was using their batter. Everybody liked the hotcakes now. Well, that was fine until there was a change of oilers. The cook couldn't figure out why suddenly nobody wanted hotcakes."

The Greek did make marvellous chicken soup, however. The crew, including Eddie, couldn't get enough of it. At home on the farm in Saanich, he mentioned this unusually tasty soup to his mother one day and she encouraged him to get the recipe. So on his next trip Eddie considered this. The cook's explosive temperament discouraged a direct request but Eddie thought that perhaps he, himself, could ferret out the ingredients. When the Greek was otherwise occupied, Eddie slipped into the galley and surreptitiously lifted the lid of the bubbling soup pot. "It was filled with chickens," said Eddie. "Whole chickens. I mean heads, feet, crap, the works." Eddie dropped the lid and fled. He became one of the very few who refused chicken soup.

The Sudbury. Seaspan

The *Sudbury* had successfully completed her first transpacific tow against considerable odds. Despite the fact that the *Straits Maru* was almost too old to remain afloat they had delivered her to her destination. Now the return journey was to be a circuitous one. Approaching the Aleutians, on the great curving route home, she was called to go to the assistance of Fred Devine's *Salvage Chief*. This vessel was towing the stern section of a Japanese freighter, the *Nozima Maru*, and was making virtually no progress. Even with the *Sudbury*'s help the two tugs could only manage $2\frac{1}{2}$ knots. It was "like dragging a big box." There were three men on the tow using pumps to keep the thing afloat but they were fighting a losing battle. As time went on the pumps were no longer keeping the ocean at bay and the salvors expressed an urgent desire to repair to higher ground. The *Sudbury*'s deck crew pulled in their wire and the tug went back to the tow. They dragged their scramble net on deck, secured it over the side, then tied two heaving lines together and waited while Harley brought the *Sudbury*'s stern in a boat-length from the tow. Now a deckhand heaved the line into the air and it arced across the water, uncoiling as it went, and landed with a thud at the salvors' feet.

Then there was a pause in the proceedings. All three men on the tow were wearing life jackets and all three were unanimous in their eagerness to vacate the premises. But the prospect of jumping 20 feet into a forbidding and frigid sea can have a dampening effect on one's enthusiasm. For moments these non-swimmers held back. "Get a move on, you guys. We're not hanging around here all day," yelled someone on the tug and finally, one after the other, the salvors tied the rope around their waists and jumped into the water. The deck crew hauled them in, and as each man reached the ship's side he climbed up the scramble nets and, teeth chattering, was hurried to the warmth of the engine room. At 10:00 that night the blip on the radar disappeared: the derelict had sunk.

This detour had used up much of the *Sudbury*'s fuel supply so she turned around and headed back to Japan to refuel. Once again she started for home and once again she was ordered to the assistance of another vessel—this one a drifting British ship, the *Arrow*. They reached her late at night. The mate, Jimmy Talbott, hauled the metal box containing the rocket gun out of its storage place in the wheelhouse and prepared to shoot a line to the other ship.

A Schermuly rocket gun is exactly that: a gun—a pistol with an extended barrel with a handle on top of that barrel. To use it, one grips the pistol grip in one hand, steadies the barrel with the other hand on the handle, aims upward at a 45-degree angle and fires. Propelled by a cartridge of gunpowder, a light line, uncoiling as it goes, can cover a distance of 175 feet. There are not fewer than four packed lines in the box, for wind, waves and general trauma are apt to interfere with the marksman's aim. Now, in the dark on the heaving stern, sometimes up to his waist in water, Jimmy Talbott fired rockets till the heaving line reached its mark and the deckhands fastened their wire to her anchor chain. They towed her to Vancouver. It was November 1956. Almost immediately they were out in the Pacific again, this time to rescue the *Thunderbird* and, before the year ended, the *Rowanmore*.

Ray Thomas was home for Christmas. It was a happy time: he had a job he thoroughly enjoyed with a company he already felt attached to, he had made close friends and felt himself very much a member of the Island Tug family. And that year he attended the first of many company Christmas parties. These were elaborate and meticulously organized affairs. There was a dinner dance for the adults and an afternoon party for the children. Each Christmas Santa arrived with due pomp and ceremony. One year the jolly old elf navigated the length of the Crystal Gardens Pool in an IT lifeboat towed by comely helpers in swimsuits. He bore a sack containing carefully chosen presents for each child. Island Tug children were acknowledged not only at Christmas but throughout the year. The parents of new arrivals received letters of congratulation and their children continued to be remembered and inquired after. This personal interest created a unique bond between employer and employees. So it was not the parties themselves that Ray especially remembered years afterwards but the fact that when H.B. appeared on stage, the entire gathering, unbidden, surged to its feet and cheered him.

Surveys relating to job satisfaction confirm that "recognition" ranks above all else on a worker's wish list. Harold Elworthy understood this and built his employee relations upon it. He knew each of his employees by name and let them know that their services were valued and that the company was always behind them. Interestingly enough, the value of their services was not necessarily measured or rewarded in monetary terms. There were, for example, no more bonuses handed out in the years that followed the rescue of the *Makedonia*.

"It always surprised me," said John Rodgers, one of the *Sudbury II*'s engineers. "I had been led to believe that when you picked ships up at sea like that there'd be some prize money. We never did get a red sou out of it. We spent five months on one trip. Compared with a local tug where we would have got day for day I'd have made more money. They were making use of my deep-sea ticket but moneywise I lost out."

There were those who complained, and even quit, over what they perceived as unfair treatment. But for every one of these there were a dozen who brushed aside such complaints. "We got piles of overtime," they explained, which seemed to be enough—piles of overtime and individual recognition.

"If some guy's wife had a flooded basement while he was away, the office sent a gang with pumps the minute she hung up the phone," said Bob MacDonald.

"When I was in hospital a huge bouquet of flowers arrived," recalled John Rodgers. "I said, 'Who in the world is that from?' and the nurse said, 'From your employer.'"

"When our first child was born Marylou was having difficulties," said Ray Thomas. "The office called John Watt and told him not to alarm me but to detour the tug into Vancouver. They said they would fly me home."

One Island Tug employee said, "Whether this kind of thing was calculated on H.B.'s part or not who knows. All I know is it was good business; it paid off."

The few who found this "Island Tug family" atmosphere too paternalistic moved on. The majority, however, repaid this company support with unswerving loyalty. "Everybody went all out for

The Sudbury *enters Vancouver harbour with the disabled* Andros Legend *in tow, 1958.* B.C. Jennings photo, Seaspan

Mr. Elworthy," said Peter Wright, the company's insurance broker.

In 1956 the *Sudbury* and her crew had gone to the aid of four ships—the *Walvis Bay*, the *Arrow*, the *Thunderbird* and the *Rowanmore*—and had brought them safely in. Island Tug & Barge was building a solid reputation in the fiercely competitive salvage business. Two years later, when the *Andros Legend* lost her propeller some 2,100 miles out of Vancouver, the *Sudbury* succeeded where her competition failed, and that reputation became unassailable.

The *Andros Legend* lay dead in the water, 1,400 miles west of Honolulu. Her owners contacted Puget Sound Tug & Barge of Seattle and arranged for their tug, the *Neptune*, to go to her assistance on a daily hire basis. But on February 25, 1958 the embattled *Neptune* reported that heavy seas had smashed her pilothouse windows, she was taking on water and was forced to return to Seattle. The *Andros Legend*'s owners approached Island Tug. The *Sudbury* had just rescued the *Lomaland* and was proceeding to Vancouver with her in tow. The *Island Sovereign* was dispatched to relieve her and the *Sudbury* turned toward the middle of the Pacific Ocean. On March 6 Harley sent the following message to Victoria: "Commenced towing at 8:15 p.m. Pacific Standard Time. Estimated date of arrival in Vancouver, subject to weather, March 21." On March 18, the *Sudbury* and her charge entered Vancouver Harbour.

Perhaps nowhere else in the world is there a larger concentration of towboat men than on the British Columbia coast. Since the early 1900s they have towed across the unprotected waters of Queen Charlotte Sound, through the ferocious tides of Seymour Narrows and down the treacherous west coast of Vancouver Island. They have towed in blankets of fog and in screaming southeasters. They have paid their dues. But they had never towed anything the size of an aircraft carrier, had never experienced a typhoon, had never switched tows in mid-Pacific. These things the Island Tug men taught themselves. These towboaters became salvors, and aside from a couple of aged barges that simply disintegrated, they never lost a tow. It was—and is—a remarkable record.

CHAPTER VI

The Tandem Tows

"And in the midst of all this I came upon an oiler who had one of the engineers by the throat."

World War II had been over for ten years and the harbours on the Pacific Coast were still choked with surplus naval vessels and Liberty ships. It took some time for this situation to come to the attention of the bureaucrats that deal with such things, and yet more time for them to form committees and send memos to each other. But by the mid-1950s they had reached the unanimous and illogical decision that there was no other destination for these ships except the scrapyards of Japan. And so a trickle became a stream and very soon deep-sea towing became a new and growing business for Island Tug.

Harold Elworthy, always quick off the mark, always poised for expansion, cast about for another deep-sea tug, and found two.

In the fall of 1958, in Australia, the company found the ships that would become the *Sudbury II* and the *Cambrian Salvor*. Built in Napa, California, they were sold to the British Admiralty and ended up being used as light plants for small communities in Australia. Now one of them, the *Cambrian Salvor*, was to be based in Yokohama; the other, the *Sudbury II*, would work out of Victoria.

Island Tug could not have found more suitable ships. The *Sudbury II* (and all these specs apply to her sister ship as well) was 214 feet long with a flared bow and an afterdeck that occupied a third of her length. She had a businesslike air about her, which was entirely fitting for she had been designed expressly for deep-sea salvage and was built to survive that most hostile of environments—a war. She was equipped for every conceivable emergency at sea. She had a large decontamination tank for the storage of used oil and a decompression chamber for divers. Her backup systems had backup systems. A ten-inch fire main ran right through the ship; in a pinch it could supply cooling for all the machinery. There was a standby lubrication system and she had a desalination plant to convert salt water to fresh. All her machinery was spring mounted so that it could endure a bomb concussion and keep on working. There was a sick bay equipped and stocked to handle a variety of medical contingencies (including minor surgery!) and there was even an extra-large electric oven in the galley for a cook who might be feeding large numbers of salvage men. She was a "quiet" ship, a way ahead of her time in noise attenuation, and she was a superb sea boat. Captain Adrian Bull recalls: "We picked up a little German ship out in the Pacific and towed her to Honolulu. When we left we came out around Diamond Head and I have never seen such big swells in my life. The swells were building as they neared the island. *Sudbury II*'s bridge was 24 feet above the water and then it was another 5 feet to eye level. You could stand on the bridge and look up at the swells. The damn boat, you could just feel her shuddering and straining to get up over the top of the swell and then she'd go wanging down the other side. She never took a drop of water on deck. Never. I stood there and watched. That ship had such a big flare. They were just great sea boats." She had only two flaws: her crew accommodation was, in George Hunter's word, "atrocious," and her engines were, in René Fournier's opinion, cursed by a fuel system that was too complex for the purpose.

"*Sudbury II* was a marvellous ship in every way except living conditions," said George Hunter. "In the winter when we went to places like Adak it was *so* cold. We had all kinds of portable heaters. And it was just as bad in summer. When we got into Japan one time Harold Elworthy came aboard. We'd been bitching bitterly about the heat and H.B.'s position was, 'Well, that's the way it is. What are you going to do? She's an old ship.' We

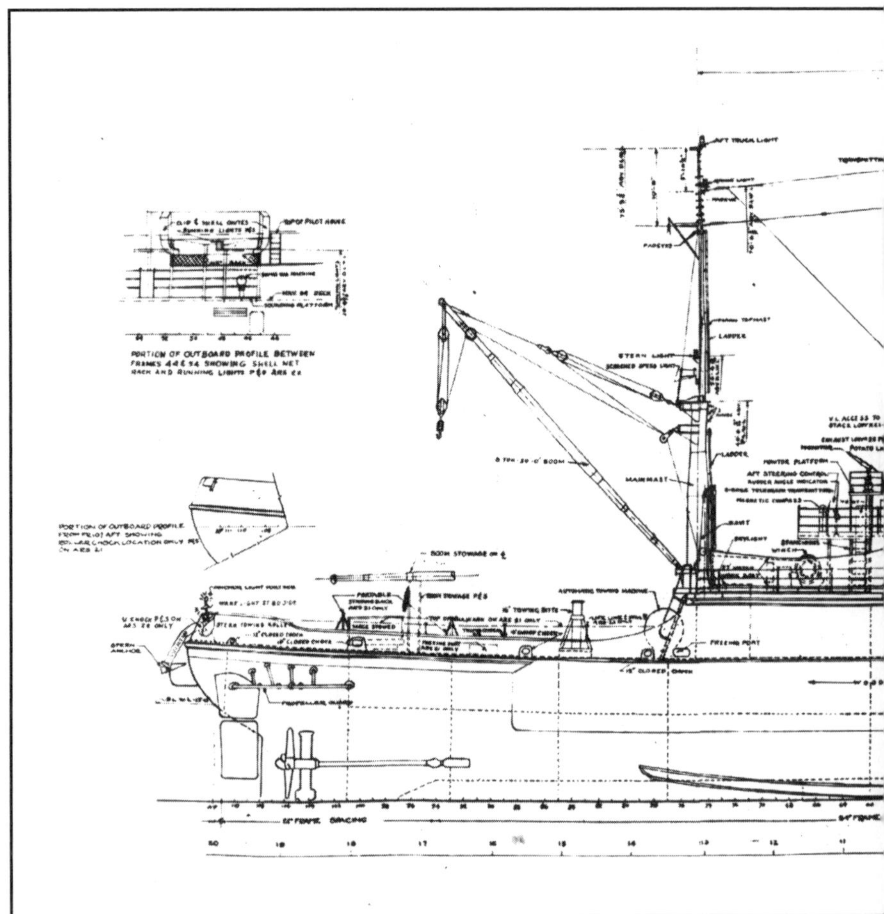

The Sudbury II*'s outboard profile.* Seaspan

managed to talk H.B. into coming down into our mess room. He got his handkerchief out and started mopping his face. He said to Harley, 'Go ashore and buy every fan you can get.'" The designers, who had put so much thought into the rest of the ship and who had possessed, in spades, that elusive skill that creates a seaworthy vessel, seemed to have lost interest when it came to living conditions. Encased in steel with no ports, no insulation and no air conditioning, the crew froze in winter and boiled in summer. One of their number, Mac Finlayson, actually got heat exhaustion while asleep in his berth, which must be a first of some sort.

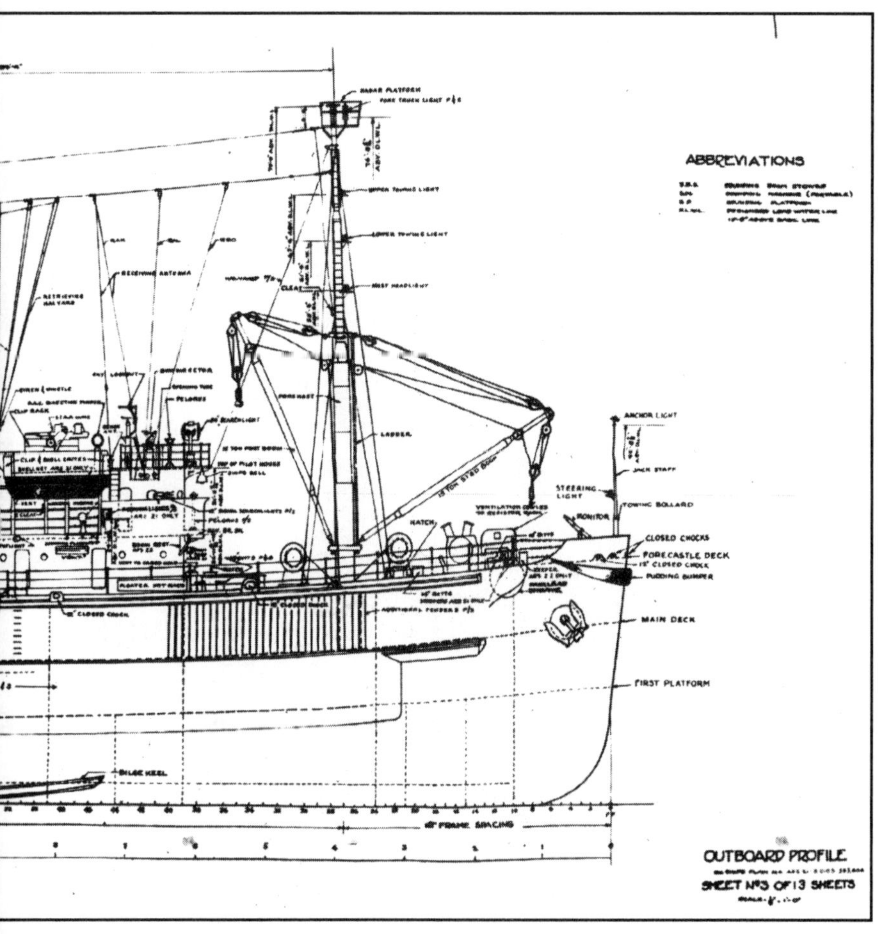

And the engines, Cooper-Bessemers, although rugged, had a complex injection system that was to plague a whole troop of engineers. There were four of these engines and one or two of them (and sometimes, to the captain's dismay, three) were frequently down. It was such a rare occurrence to have them all working at the same time that once, when Harry Sapro was Chief and he entered the mess room—all four engines thrumming beneath him—he was startled to find himself cheered by the assembled company.

The Sudbury II *entering Victoria harbour, still sporting her wartime grey paint.* William Boucher photo, Seaspan

Harley Blagborne, having made Island Tug's name with the first *Sudbury*, was given command of the *Sudbury II*. He and his crew flew down to Australia in October 1958 to bring her home. Her sterling qualities hidden under grime and neglect, she didn't, at first, impress her new crew. For weeks they laboured away to get her in shape and on their one and only day off they all trooped off to the Sydney zoo.

Island Tug was not a company to chintz. The *Sudbury II*, refitted once in Australia, was refitted all over again on her return to Victoria because her Chief Engineer's low opinion of Australian workmanship had been confirmed on the trip back.

Finally put into acceptable shape, she became one of the links in a shuttle service to the Japanese breakup yards. Back and forth across the Pacific the two *Sudbury*s, the *Cambrian Salvor* and sometimes the *Island Sovereign*, as well, performed a kind of relay race. The *Sudbury* brought the tows as far as the Hawaiian Islands where they were transferred to the *Sudbury II* or the *Cambrian Salvor* to complete the voyage to Japan. The first ship then refuelled and returned for the next tow.

On the way to Japan, c. 1959. George N.Y. Simpson photo, Seaspan

If these tows to the scrapyards conjure up the vision of a procession of rusty hulks, that's an inaccurate picture. The US Navy mothballed with meticulous care and some of the ships the *Sudbury*s towed were in brand-new condition, or were in fact brand new. Sometimes the *Sudbury*s' crews stared in wonder at machinery that had never turned a wheel and was now to be scrapped. Indeed, they reflected, some of this "scrap" was in better shape than the ships they were sent out to salvage. All emergencies generate waste, however, and war is the ultimate emergency, so these observers shrugged their shoulders, coupled up the tows and set off across the Pacific, knowing that this waste was at least providing them with a livelihood.

With this steady supply of off-shore business came the need for more captains with deep-sea tickets. Suddenly Island Tug was hiring captains who weren't towboat men and never had been. They came from Great Britain, Ireland, Malta and Norway. They brought with them ocean-going tickets which meant they had the ability to navigate a vast open ocean. What they *didn't* bring with them was any experience with towing gear or small-boat handling. The merging of deep-sea experience with coastal towing skills was initially a difficult transition for them. George Hunter was an example: "When I started," he said, "I had never landed a boat in my life." Some of them became adept at this new skill; some left it to their mates. Steve Fairhurst, one of the old guard, could make a boat talk. Watching one of these newcomers attempt a landing reduced Steve to incoherent snorts. And each captain had a different idea of what constitutes safety. It's an old saying: "The coastal man is scared when he gets out of sight of land and the deep-sea man is scared when he gets into sight of land." Steve Fairhurst and Adrian Bull once got into this tug-of-war in a storm at the north end of Unimak Pass.

"We can get in here, we'll go in there," said Steve, happy to see clusters of offshore islands.

"No, no, we'll go a bit farther outside," said the deep-sea skipper, viewing these same islands with alarm.

George Hunter, one of these new captains, had emigrated from England in 1957; with his foreign-going master's ticket he was able to get a job in the Arctic and make a stake. He and his wife put a down payment on a house and George settled into a job as a school janitor. But then, in the summer of 1959, he got a call from the Merchant Service Guild: "Want to go to Japan? Island Tug needs a mate with a foreign-going ticket." Janitoring doesn't do much for the soul. George packed his things and headed for Victoria. The first thing he did was breeze into Island Tug's offices.

"Name's George Hunter. I'd like an advance on my wages."

The fellow in the office looked dumbfounded.

"Look," George explained, "I don't know anything about towboats or towboat companies but when you go deep-sea in Britain you can get an advance."

The clerk, not yet used to anything but coastal towing, hemmed and hawed for a few minutes but George left with his advance. His towboat career had begun.

It began, to be exact, on July 14, 1959. On the *Sudbury II*'s stern and on the bows of two hulking Liberty ships the deck crew, using their winch, coupled chain to towing wire with shackles the size of automobile wheels and then welded their nuts into place. Wrestling with 80-pound shackles and 11 tons of towing wire, one of the men was hurt. Loath to delay their departure, Harley sent him off for medical attention and plucked a replacement, Don Tetreault, off one of the little Island Tug harbour tugs. That morning Don had bidden his wife goodbye and gone off to his job wearing a T-shirt and jeans and carrying his lunch bucket. Thus, scantily prepared, he was now on his way to Japan. Early in the afternoon the dispatcher phoned Mrs. Tetreault.

The Sudbury II*'s shackles were the size of automobile wheels.*
Sheret photo, Seaspan

"Just to tell you Don won't be home for supper, Mrs. Tetreault."

"And when shall I expect him?"

"Not for a while, actually. He's gone to Japan."

She was furious, the man recalled. "That marriage didn't last too long," he said. "She was a very religious woman." What religion had to do with it is hard to see.

Like Ray Thomas before him, George Hunter found that Harley was happy to leave the navigating to anyone qualified so George plotted their way across the Pacific on the Great Circle Route. He remembers, "Once Harley knew you could navigate, he left it to you. The proudest day of my life was the day we picked up the *Guadalcanal* because he was adrift and there was a US destroyer standing by him till we got there. I told Harley, 'Well, we're here. They should be here.' And we found him in half an hour."

On this trip they arrived at their destination, Tokuyama, late on August 26. Next morning they would deliver their tow to the breakup yards. Now, around them, Japan's Inland Sea lay as smooth and black as polished ebony. At midnight George went up to the pilothouse to relieve his captain.

"Well, there you are," said Harley. "I've got them on a short line. Just cut doughnuts all night."

"What d'you mean?"

"Just keep going all night."

"I've never heard of anything like this in my bloody life," said George. His face must have shown his incomprehension, for the helmsman, Georgie Webb, explained, "You keep going and you don't go too tight, because if you do you'll hit the towline, so just keep going in a big circle, slow speed, and you'll be all right."

"This guy doesn't know anything about towboating," said Harley to Georgie, "but this is his chance to learn."

Right on both counts, thought George. Jokingly referred to as "that red-headed Commie," George Hunter has the fiery temperament that matches his hair and he's the first to admit that his intemperate words have occasionally caused him trouble. And, if he wasn't a communist, he was certainly a socialist. As such he had little use for the artificial boundaries that separated the officers and crew, the black gang and the deck crew, the oil and water that don't mix. He had always held to the view that they needed each other—that they, quite literally, sank or swam together.

George and René Fournier, the third engineer, had the same watch. They spent their coffee breaks together each night; sitting on benches in the mess room they solved all the problems of the world. It was during these mug-ups that George realized just how isolated the black gang were and how little they knew—or saw—of what was going on above their heads. And so it was George who was responsible for one of the pictures that has stayed in René's mind for forty years. Dawn had brought a bank of fog. The voice pipe in the engine room whistled and it was George.

"You'd better take a run out on deck. You'll see something you've probably never seen before."

René went out on deck and there, spread before him, was a living replica of the Japanese flag. An enormous sun rose out of the sea circled by huge golden rays that filled the sky. René stood there, overwhelmed. On the sea hundreds of small Japanese fishing boats dotted the water, making the whole scene a picture out of *Sinbad the Sailor*. René went down into the engine room.

"You'd better go up on deck," he told the oilers, "because I don't know how many times in your life you'll see Japan's rising sun."

The *Sudbury II* dropped her tow in Hirao and most of the crew, all fellows in their teens and twenties, rushed off to see the sights of Japan. Not so the black gang. Thinking back, René Fournier says that the name *Sudbury II* is inextricably associated in his mind with the word "work." He worked so hard and so continuously that in a month and a half he had worn out a brand-new pair of boots. And this work didn't stop when they reached port. Long-range towing means boredom on the upper decks while below the wear and tear becomes more demanding of attention as the running time accumulates. So there were no breaks for the "black gang" who toiled away doing repairs, which was a bit ironic, as far as René Fournier was concerned. He had started his working life driving a cat for a logging show. Four thousand feet up on a sidehill, his boss came along and told him to take the cat down to the bottom road.

"It'll take me a while to get down there," said René, eyeing the switchbacks below him.

"Not long, just drop her down."

"What?"

"Just drop her down on the cable with your winch."

"You expect me to winch this thing down there?"

"Well, if you can't do it I'll get somebody else."

"So," René said later, "I hung on that thing like a spider, let her go, lowered myself till I came up against a stump, unhooked the other end and brought her back in and hooked it onto that stump and kept going down. I looked down and I thought, Oh, boy. I didn't feel all that great about it, I'll tell you that. I thought, I hope this winch is in good shape, because if it all lets go I'm headed down into the straits.

"But it was on this job that I first thought about going towboating. Working way up on that sidehill the tugs and booms down below in the straits were so small—and they never seemed to go at more than a snail's pace. Must be a good job, I said to myself, they don't *do* anything. Little did I know—the machinery on them was red-hot just trying to make that little bit of distance."

Now he was not only working his guts out, he thought ruefully, but was struggling, like all the rest of the black gang, with four unfamiliar Cooper-Bessemer engines. They had manuals for all this complex machinery, but these had been designed for military use and kept referring to "flank output," which meant "flat out" and was about as far from towing requirements as one could get. Still, young and full of enthusiasm, they persevered, proceeding by trial and error and modifying their approach as they went. They found that the complicated and finicky fuel injectors were the weak point and that trying to detect which one was causing the trouble took more time than it was worth. So eventually when they had injector problems they just yanked them *all* out—and got so good at it that they could do it in half an hour.

The job was tough for another reason, as well. The *Sudbury II* was a fine ship but she had been neglected, which meant that things were forever going wrong. The auxiliary kept blowing its pistons and spewing black grease all over the deck crews' fresh paint; the bolts holding the injectors in place were all mismatched and required a fistful of wrenches; the problems were never-ending. Yet these neophytes never lost their enthusiasm, day after day slogging away with the best will in the world. It was just as well that they did, for there were further tests to come.

Working the shuttle service meant long months at sea so that the *Sudbury II*, which had left Victoria in July, was still out in mid-Pacific in October. Each time their return to Victoria was delayed, Mrs. Hunter, expecting her first child, was reduced to tears. Alone in a new country, far from her family and friends in England and from her husband out on the Pacific Ocean, she was hard put to keep her spirits up.

Off the coast of Japan, her husband was equally anxious to get home, but that didn't seem imminently likely for he was heading eastward, not westward. The *Sudbury II* had just switched tows with the *Sudbury* off the Hawaiian Islands and was returning to Japan with two more Liberty ships. It was now hurricane season and on October 14 the *Sudbury II* received the weather forecast they had been half-expecting for weeks: the warning of an impending typhoon, dubbed Charlotte. In the tug's wheelhouse Harley tracked the storm's path and altered course but the typhoon altered course as well. The abstract reads:

October 14	slight to rough sea, low swells, periods of heavy rain, reduced speed for engine repairs
15	reduce speed account typhoon Charlotte, rough sea, heavy swell
16	evasive course, anticipated course of Charlotte dangerous
17	vessel endeavoring to evade path of Charlotte, rough sea, heavy swell
18	reports on Charlotte's path erratic, vessel attempting to run out of right hand semi-circle, very rough following sea, very heavy swell
19	vessel in typhoon, running before weather in the right hand semi-circle, hove-to left hand semi-circle, heavy to phenomenal swells, very rough seas, violent squalls

Their attempt to evade the storm had failed. Now all they could do was put up lifelines, make everything secure and endure what was to come.

The young male is short on experience, seduced by risk and convinced of his immortality—all characteristics that predisposed the younger members of the crew to view the prospect of a typhoon with some enthusiasm. The exception was the electrician; in a former life this non-seaman had had "some sort of a nervous breakdown" and it had been suggested that a sea voyage would be the ideal thing for him. Unfortunately the people who make these kinds of suggestions seldom have any idea what a sea voyage entails. Now as the wind increased, so did this man's terror. Facing one towering sea after the other the *Sudbury II* creaked, groaned and shuddered. In the engine room the cooling system alarms set off shrill cries of panic. Like Eddie Gait before him, the electrician felt it unlikely that a ship could take a beating like this and survive. He struggled to his cabin, went inside, locked the door, got down on his knees and began to pray. The *Sudbury II* took another wild lunge and threw him onto the deck, sending a searing pain through one elbow. From that position the electrician continued his efforts to contact God.

At midnight George clawed his way up to the wheelhouse to relieve Harley. The wind had suspended so much water in the air that everything outside the windows was obscured, as in a fog.

"Here you are," said Harley. "I don't know where the tows are. I can't see them—too much clutter on the radar. I just hope to hell we're in front of them and not the other way around."

At 1:30 a.m. the wind died completely. For two hours there was only the thrumming of the engines. The *Sudbury II*, water running off her from stem to stern, shook herself and waited, but not for long. At 3:00 a.m. the wind burst upon them just as suddenly as it had left and continued to tear at them for the next three days.

In the engine room it was "all hands available." René Fournier recalled: "We were expecting it. We were told to make sure that everything was well lashed down. We were told to be prepared for the worst. This was a vessel with almost legendary sea-keeping abilities but still we weren't prepared for what happened.

"The Chief Engineer and I were in the machine shop; we were having a cigarette with our butts against the work bench. We were talking about how well we had everything tied down—how we had everything under control. Suddenly we took one hell of a roll and a lathe chuck flew out of its holder and whizzed past our ears.

"We thought, Jesus, holy Moses, if this is what it's going to be like... Christ.

"Well, it didn't stop. That was just the beginning; it was like that for hours. And all hell was breaking loose in the engine room because this was a shallow draft vessel so it was clearing its suction. This was really a bad situation because the engines started to overheat. We were going from engine to engine, shutting them down, clearing the air out of the system, and firing them up again—and by that time another one would fail. This went on and on and on and now with the stirring up of the dirt in the fuel tanks, the fuel filters started plugging up. It was a madhouse. Due to the vessel's sojourn in Australia the fuel filters didn't have two bolts that were the same size. Nobody had recognized this as a problem but now in all this noise and confusion everyone was trying to get the right-sized wrench from everyone else. And in the midst of all this I came upon an oiler who's got one of the engineers by the throat. I thought, Uh-oh, this is a personal thing, and I just kind of slid by. I guess this engineer hadn't been too polite about something.

"This was all happening in the middle of the night, and you have to bear in mind now that nobody was in bed. Everybody was working—everybody was running around trying to keep the machinery going. We had all lost track of time but at some point in the middle of all this, water started coming down through the vents onto one of our generators. The vents had a device for keeping water out but one of these had been inadvertently left unsecured. And so the Chief came to me and said, 'You've got to go up there and fix that.'"

"I said, 'Are you crazy? Send someone from the deck crew.'"

"'Sorry,' he said. 'You're the only one who knows how to do this.'"

"And unfortunately he was right, because I had been on the

ship since Australia and I was the only one that was familiar with these things. I wasn't very happy about this because, first of all, I don't swim. But I got some tools and thought, Okay, well, I guess that's the way it is.

"What I remember is that it was like going into—or out of—a chamber. These two deckhands opened the door for me, yelled, 'Way you go!' and I could hear the bolts slamming shut behind me.

"I stood there collecting myself, and as my night vision began to focus I registered an amazing sensation. I was watching a wall of water going right up past me like a mountain. I couldn't figure it out. I was totally disoriented. And then the mountain would recede and disappear over the side of the ship. I had a lifeline and I snapped it onto the ship's lifeline and had enough slack to get to the side of the ship. Because now this fascinated me. The ship's qualities were such that we weren't hammering; it was just a very long long roll. So I got to the ship's side because it just absolutely fascinated me; there was no more fear about this, I was just fascinated. I had to know what was going on here. What was going on was that we were rolling so far that as we rolled into it the water appeared to be coming past till the horizon was up in the air somewhere—and then of course the water would totally disappear under the ship as I looked down past it. I thought, My God, no wonder we're having troubles down below.

"With that I totally lost my fear. It made such an impression to actually see what was happening up here. The people in the engine room never knew what was going on outside—in the sense of how much water was flying around. We were just so busy doing what we were doing that we were certainly not going to go up on the bridge and say, 'Can I see what's happening up here?'

"So having seen this I was very very impressed and I will never forget that; I will *never* forget the extent that we were rolling. And no wonder we couldn't keep things going normally down below. However we did very well. We did exceedingly well under the circumstances because everybody was really working hard."

For George Hunter, Island Tug's new deep-sea mate, a typhoon was not a new experience, although George could never have imagined *towing* in such conditions. For the coastwise members of the crew, "ignorant kids" like Eddie Gait, the typhoon was a sharp reminder that they were in the big leagues now, where carelessness, inattention or simple laziness could endanger everyone on the ship. They emerged from the experience more confident in the *Sudbury II* and in themselves. In Bob Gray's words, they had "sledded her out." They had, indeed.

CHAPTER VII

The *Fanshaw Bay*

"Tell them f— all; they're the competition."

The procession of scrap ships now leaving the west coast for Japan was carefully prepared for the long trip across the anything but pacific Pacific. One of the first steps in this preparation was the removal of their propellers, which reduced the tow's drag considerably. That first frustrating attempt to saw off the propeller of the *Icotea* in the Caribbean had taught the Island Tug crews what they needed to know and by this time they had the procedure down pat. They flooded the forward end of the ship in order to tip up the stern and then the *Skookum*, a steam derrick mounted on a scow, came alongside and moored at the stern. The *Skookum* carried several bottles of propane on deck and one of these was connected to a 3-foot length of 3/8-inch steel pipe. Used as a primitive cutting torch, this sliced through a 12-inch shaft in no time at all. Meanwhile a wire sling was attached to the propeller itself so that when it was free of the shaft the *Skookum*'s derrick could lift it onto the deck of the ship.

By and large this job was handled by Jack Daly, Island Tug's diver, and his tenderman, Jake Derksen. Daly modelled himself on John Wayne, and to some extent his big frame and craggy features did resemble those of the western movie star. His personality, however was entirely his own; he was obstinate, opinionated and abrasive. When a salvage job required them to travel to the site by truck, Jack always insisted on driving. The salvage master of the time, Jack McLaughlin, insisted equally vehemently that he wouldn't sit beside him. Jake became the buffer, and sometimes their quarrelling was almost too much for him. "One of these days," Jake told H.B., "I'm just going to get out and hitchhike back." Nor was Jack hesitant about self-promotion; he was a consummate showman. Flamboyance and showmanship were not what earned him his employer's respect, however. He was valued because he was a diver who could—and would—do anything. His feats were legendary. "He was rough and tough," said Adrian Bull. "Just the kind of guy you want."

Jake Derksen was a former logger. When fire season closed the woods one summer, Jake heard that Island Tug was looking for a rigger for a two-week job at Clo-oose and he applied. Island Tug had a reputation for taking on difficult jobs and this was one of them. H.B.'s approach was to get the job first and figure out how to do it afterwards. This one involved righting an enormous barge and it fell to Norman Turner to figure out how to do it. Norman had a special winch built and two A-frames constructed and they were towed to the site. Jake rigged the A-frames and ran the winch and "the barge flipped over pretty damn nice." When he got back to Victoria he found he had a permanent job—and it lasted for thirty-one years. He learned the job of diver's tender and picked up many other useful skills, including the ability to take the propellers off a string of ships bound for the scrap yard.

In early January of 1960, Hill Wilson joined this parade across the Pacific. His telephone rang and it was the Island Tug dispatcher.

"How about a trip to Japan, Hill?"

Captain Hill Wilson is a tall, immaculately tailored man with the crisp, authoritative manner that his profession demands. But behind the brisk manner lurks an Irish warmth and wit. If the subtle sense of humour is cultural in origin, then both the tailoring and the authority are no doubt the result of his training at St. Margaret's College, Nova Scotia—an institution that once turned out officers for the Canadian Merchant Marine. Hill had made many trips to Japan on Canadian Pacific ships and on Park ships, but now he was an Island Tug captain and the only Island Tug vessels that sailed to Japan were the two *Sudbury*s and the *Sovereign*.

"Want you to bring back the *Sudbury II*," continued the dispatcher.

"What about Harley?" said Hill. The *Sudbury II* was, of course, Harley Blagborne's ship.

"Harley's fine. He's over in Tokyo, that's the problem. His wife is going to have a baby. She's going to have an operation or something on the 13th and she says we'd better get Harley back here right now or we're going to be short one captain."

"Right you are," said Hill, and headed for Japan.

The *Sudbury II* returned to the west coast light, which gave her new captain a chance to become familiar with his command. By February the vessel was back in Victoria preparing for the next tow: an aircraft carrier named the *Fanshaw Bay*, which they were to pick up in Astoria.

If Hill Wilson had never laid eyes on the *Fanshaw Bay* he would probably have more hair than he has today. There's no scientific basis for this speculation, of course, because we all know that we are able to propel a man into space but we haven't as yet mastered the ability to keep his hair attached to his head. Still, it's an undeniable fact that Hill had much more hair at the beginning of the voyage than he had at the end of it, and the *Fanshaw Bay* must bear some of the responsibility. Dragging something the size of a twenty-storey building across the Pacific through a series of typhoons ages those involved.

In Astoria the deck crew connected their towing gear to this monster and took on a Columbia River pilot—a man who was eighty if a day and had a cavalier attitude when it came to towing.

"Half Ahead," he ordered, barely clear of their moorings.

The Fanshaw Bay *looming astern the* Sudbury II, *1960.* Seaspan

"Like hell," cried Hill, grabbing for the telegraph.

After this rocky start, they came to an arrangement: the pilot would be in charge of their direction and Hill would specify how they got there.

This division of duty decided, the *Sudbury II* and her tow gained the open Pacific and headed for Victoria, where the carrier was to be made ready for the coming trip. It was apparent right from the very beginning, however, that this tow was assuming a character all its own. When they reached that port a gale was blowing and, unable to manoeuvre their unwieldy charge in close quarters, they steamed around in circles out in the strait. There were still Fleet Air Arm aircraft stationed at Patricia Bay at this time and their pilots found the unexpected appearance of an aircraft carrier too great a temptation to resist. The crew of the *Sudbury II* watched in astonishment as the airmen staged a series of mock landings on their tow.

In Victoria both vessels were prepared for the trip ahead. Welders patched holes in the hull of the *Fanshaw Bay* where piping had been removed; on the *Sudbury II* engineers laboured over her engines and the tug was bunkered and provisioned. Then, on February 19, both tug and tow were finally declared ready for the open sea and they began the long voyage across the Pacific.

As it happened, few of Hill Wilson's crew had any towboat experience nor did he himself have a great deal. One of the deckhands was actually a carpenter and the first mate had spent his career on deep-sea ships. The second mate had worked ashore for many years and was simply anxious to get in enough sea time to qualify as a captain (and to be addressed as such). After his years ashore this trip was to prove a severe shock to the man's system. One of the oilers had *never* been to sea before and the combination of rolling and pitching and diesel fumes was his undoing. The Chief was dying of lung cancer, a burden that made coping with the idiosyncrasies of the unfamiliar Cooper-Bessemers almost more than the poor man could bear. Fortunately Hill had a rare and valuable skill: the knack of knowing how to treat each individual man to get what he wanted out of him. "Hill took the offensive," one of the crew said. "He came aboard very much the captain. In two hours he had everybody eating out of his hand—even those who had professed their dislike of him."

Ten days out of Victoria, in deteriorating weather, this crew encountered their first test. They were having dinner when a sudden heavy jerk signalled that the *Sudbury II* was no longer connected to the *Fanshaw Bay*. Hauling a towline in will answer the question of where the break occurred and it will sometimes supply the answer to why it broke. As the deck crew winched in half a mile of wire, both questions were answered: a link connecting the pennant to the chain was rusted and it had fractured.

The carrier had been rigged with an auxiliary pickup towing line. A 1-inch line, it was made fast to a wire pennant at the bow and ran aft along the flight deck. It was secured with light fastenings and at the stern it hung down over the flight deck to within a couple of feet of the water. Now the *Sudbury II* backed in under the carrier's looming bulk and snatched the end of the line. Pulling the fastenings free she connected herself once more to her tow. This temporary towing gear wasn't up to the rigours of the Pacific, however, so when the weather moderated the tug came alongside to rerig the main towing gear.

Three chain bridles hung from the carrier's bow and were connected to a 40-foot length of chain, almost all of which hung down below the surface of the water. The *Sudbury II*'s deck crew marked off 30 feet of wire with seizing and put a shackle on the end of it. Then a deckhand worked the wire around the chain with a pike pole and caught the bight in the shackle, forming a loop that could be lowered down the chain. Hill had given very clear instructions that the wire was to be lowered until it reached the 30-foot mark and then cinched up. They would then be able to haul the whole thing aboard and shackle the two together properly. They followed their captain's instructions and the first part of the procedure went like clockwork despite the tug's pitching. In half an hour they had prepared the wire, looped it around the chain and lowered it 30 feet. And then, for some inexplicable reason, the deckhand continued to lower it until it fell off the end of the chain. Hill resisted the strong temptation to throw the man right in after it, and the crew began the whole process all over again. And this time it took five hours to complete it, the tug manoeuvring constantly to keep in position. Periodically the carrier's starboard anchor reminded them of its presence by striking the *Sudbury II*'s bulwarks with disconcerting force.

Once more reconnected, they headed into the area of the Pacific which could be described as the Bermuda Triangle of Japan. Monstrous weather systems howled out of China and along the coast of Japan and then swept up east–northeast toward North America. Force 12 winds battered the tug; 3 feet of water sluiced down her decks.

Sitting in a row on an old sofa in the mess, the deck crew tried to relax with their cigarettes. The battered leather sofa was the mess room's one amenity. Except for the tabletops and benches, every surface in the room was metal. Nor was this spartan industrial decor enlivened by windows or ports. Except for its size, the mess room looked like nothing so much as the interior of a submarine. As far as the black gang were concerned, it might as well have been a submarine. For them, days went by unmarked by dawns or darkness. For the cook, working always in ample but artificial light, there was a glimpse of the outside world when he dumped the garbage. And for the ship's cat, the steel environment must have denied a deep need, for when he was taken ashore and discovered upholstery he went berserk, clawing at it in a pent-up frenzy. This claustrophobic accommodation had been designed for a purpose, of course: to keep the ship watertight. Once the doors were dogged shut, the fury of the sea was held at bay.

The aircraft carrier's steering engine had been welded into position and wires and turnbuckles were added to keep the rudder in a fore and aft position, but the heavy weather broke all these fastenings away and the rudder went hard astarboard. Now they were towing a ship that was 35 degrees off the starboard quarter. Instead of following docilely behind, the *Fanshaw Bay* was now looking over the *Sudbury II*'s shoulder. Her vast bulk caught the wind like a sail and she proceeded to drag the *Sudbury II* backwards at a steady 2 knots—not only backwards, but broadside. Periodically the *Sudbury II* would resume her authority and head into the seas once again, but only for a short time before the whole process repeated itself. The crew measured the distance travelled each day and on one record occasion found that they had made 67 miles—in the wrong direction! Ray Thomas explains this recurring phenomenon: "You can't really heave to because you have to keep tension on the towline. Oh, when you're out in heavy weather you're towing full speed and you're going backwards. You're not even hove-to. We've lost miles—just drifted backwards—just screaming out there—smoking white."

For two and a half weeks the wind howled relentlessly. It was impossible to get more than snatches of sleep. Hill Wilson's bunk was athwartships which meant that he could never lie down but rather alternated between standing on his feet and on his head. Finally, in an attempt to get some rest, he lay on the deck in his cabin between the desk and the settee and hooked his arm around the leg of the desk.

On the bridge the inclinometer registered rolls up to 57 degrees, at which point Hill and the helmsman exchanged inquiring looks.

"She always comes back," said Hill with a certainty he didn't feel.

"So you say," said the helmsman, unconvinced.

The Sudbury *towing a Liberty ship to Japan. Just the top of the tow's mast shows above the waves.* Seaspan

John Rodgers, the *Sudbury II*'s second engineer, said, "It was an experience to watch those seas. So monstrous you can hardly imagine—40 or 50 feet high. The *Sudbury II* rode up one side and disappeared down the other. Behind her the towing wire disappeared into the side of a green mountain. You rarely saw the tow. If you didn't panic it was a fantastic feeling." But as an engineer John was only too aware of the occurrences that could turn this "fantastic feeling" into a nightmare. "Your port side would probably air lock and by the time we were fighting to get the air out by opening air cocks, next thing you knew the siren was screaming its head off because the starboard side had got air locked," he said. "I can remember spending my whole watch—my whole six hours—skittling from one side of the engine room to the other, getting rid of the air locks. This was one of our main problems because we didn't want to shut off any main engines. We were keeping our fingers crossed that we didn't have a power failure. The idea of losing power in such hostile conditions was unthinkable. If we had done so we would have been gone. The tow could have overrun us. With all that shuddering and banging you never know. All it takes is some connection that isn't 100 percent, some relay to jump out. I was thinking why didn't we have automatic air bleeds on the coolers. Like you do on a house heating system, for instance. I don't know why we didn't, unless it was a design flaw. I guess they never assumed you were going to get in a typhoon."

Indeed, the black gang had their hands full. The seas had stirred up the sediment in the fuel tanks and the filters were continually clogging up. In two weeks the engineers had used up a year's supply of filters. In desperation they had taken to spinning the clogged filters in Varsol so that they could be reused. Now the dirty fuel was causing the generator to falter and the lights to go out. John was off watch. "He was in bed," said Bob Gray, "but he wasn't sleeping, I guess. When the lights started going out he realized he'd better come on down and help. There he was in his shorts trying to get the generator going." The Cooper-Bessemers were sucking air instead of cooling water and each time the pumps lost their prime, sirens screamed and lights flashed. "It was just terrible confusion," said Bob.

John Rodgers agreed. "It was quite hair-raising," he said. "Well, if anything had happened, that's the end. You'd never get a boat away in that lot."

In the galley the cook struggled to the side with the garbage, threw it overboard and watched in dismay as it floated off *ahead* of the vessel. How in the hell are we ever going to get there at this rate, Hill thought to himself. On a previous job in the Arctic he had contracted some kind of digestive trouble. These unending gales did nothing to improve this condition; he subsisted on barley water and his hair fell out in alarming quantities.

Young Bob MacDonald, the mess boy, was probably weathering the nightmare voyage as well as anyone. On a previous voyage the "mess boy" was a middle-aged acquaintance of H.B.'s, who had recently lost his wife and was finding bereavement difficult. H.B. suggested that an ocean voyage might provide a distraction and since the man had no nautical experience the job of cook's helper seemed the most suitable. However, this unfortunate man found that being confined to a heaving galley with a mean-tempered alcoholic cook did nothing to alleviate his depression, and when the ship finally docked he was the first ashore. Bob MacDonald took his place. Now, braced with his back against the bulwarks, he watched a whole ham fly off the galley counter onto the deck where it rolled back and forth, across and around with the swearing cook in hot pursuit. Finally the cook cornered it, captured it and slammed it back on the countor. Out of the corner of his eye he saw Bob watching him and smirking.

"You want some ham?" he snarled.

The weeks of fearful weather had done nothing for the Cooper-Bessemers. Sucking air into their cooling water and choking on the debris in the fuel tanks, they broke down with monotonous regularity. Struggling just to keep their feet, let alone work, the engineers fought a twenty-four-hour-a-day battle that appeared to have no end. For the Chief, who was fighting a solitary battle with a terminal illness, it was all too much. He had neither the will nor the energy to meet the challenge that these engines posed. As the *Sudbury II* approached the island of Oshima south of Yokohama in Tokyo Bay, he appeared on the bridge. He was very near to tears. "Captain," he said, "three of our engines have failed and I can't guarantee the fourth."

There was nothing to do but head for the nearest port. The

SUDBURY II

The Sudbury II, *her paint beaten off by storms, brings in the* Guadalcanal, *1959.* Captain Hill Wilson photo

Sudbury II, crawling along at 3 knots, made for Yokohama while her engineers worked feverishly to get another engine going, for in order to pull in the towline they needed at least two. The *Sudbury II*'s black gang again proved their resourcefulness. A second engine coughed to life, the deck crew shortened the towline and Hill found an anchorage in Tokyo Bay. They dropped the carrier's anchor and then their own. That night, for the first time in weeks, these exhausted seamen had a few hours of peaceful sleep.

The battered appearance of their ship attested to the gruelling trip they had all endured. Her metamorphosis was startling: their handsome ship had only vestiges of her paint work left; dwarfed by her towering charge she looked battle-scarred and weary.

The engines were repaired and a crane was hired to haul in the *Fanshaw Bay*'s anchor. With this small pause to give them a second wind, they headed for Osaka. As they approached that harbour in the dark, Hill discovered that the propane sidelights on the carrier had burned out. This hulking monster, not directly behind the tug as approaching vessels might expect but still hanging off the starboard side, now presented no lights to mark her unexpected position. A steamer approached the *Sudbury II*, and in a desperate attempt to call attention to his tow Hill turned his searchlight on the carrier.

"Run up top," he said to Jimmy Yates, "and turn on the big light."

Minutes later his inexperienced mate was back.

"Where's the switch?"

"Oh, forget it. It's too damn late," said Hill wearily, wondering if this interminable voyage would ever end.

But it did: exactly forty days and fifteen hours after their departure from Victoria, the crew dropped their anchor in Osaka's harbour. The *Fanshaw Bay* had been delivered to her destination. Through week after week of howling gales they had pressed doggedly on, and now at last they were free of the carrier's gigantic presence. The crew gave a collective sigh of exhaustion and relief.

And then two small Japanese gentlemen presented themselves: one a representative of the Japanese scrap dealer, the other his interpreter. Where, they wanted to know, was the second anchor.

"The second anchor?"

"Aircraft carrier has two anchors. We have one," the interpreter said.

"I have no idea where the other anchor is," said Hill. "I have no idea what your agreement says. You'll have to discuss this with the people at the other end."

The gentlemen showed no signs of leaving. Despite the fact that a 10-ton anchor is not an easy thing to steal—or to hide—they began looking around suspiciously.

"I assure you," said Hill, "that I am just too damned tired to even *consider* stealing an anchor."

Island Tug vessels continued to crisscross the Pacific, towing either two Liberty ships or an aircraft carrier. Sometimes they completed the entire trip, as Hill Wilson did with the *Fanshaw Bay*; more often they switched tows somewhere off the Hawaiian Islands. But before they could switch tows, they had to find each other out in that vast ocean. Ray Thomas was now mate on the *Sovereign* and he was doing the navigating.

A tandem tow: the Sudbury *leaving San Francisco with an aircraft carrier.*
Seaspan

"We left Hawaii at 9:00 a.m. to rendezvous with *Sudbury*. We got a noon position the following day and then I figured that by six o'clock that night, if we just kept going north, we would be on latitude 33. Then we altered 90 degrees to go east and I called Steve Fairhurst on the *Sudbury* on the radio. It was dusk."

"You've got to be there somewhere ahead of us, Steve."

"Oh, I don't think so. I think we've gone past you. We'll try and take a DF on you."

"Just wait till it gets really dark here," said Ray, "and you put your searchlight up to the sky and we'll see if we can see you."

In the tropics the dark came quickly. "Okay, try her now," said Ray.

Steve snapped on his light and pointed it into the overcast sky. There was the *Sudbury*, dead ahead. Ray and his pupil Jim Derby performed a jubilant high five.

At first the tugs switched tows by coming alongside to pick up the towing gear but proximity is dangerous in the open ocean. Once, early on, a wave picked up the *Sudbury II* and threatened to carry her right on top of the *Sovereign*; if the larger vessel hadn't reacted instantly and gone full astern, they would have sustained serious damage—and this on a relatively calm day. So Otto Alcorn, the *Sovereign*'s skipper, devised a better system. As the two ships motored along, the tug that was picking up the tow went ahead and passed a line to the bow of the tug behind. Then, 75 feet ahead, going dead slow, the first tug would in effect be towing the second plus the tow. The first tug's towline was then taken back to the stern of the second vessel where it was shackled to the pennant, which was fastened to the deck with a device called a Senhouse slip. When the towline was secured, the Senhouse slip was knocked off. The pennant, towline attached, slipped overboard and the first tug peeled away—at least in theory. One of the difficulties that hadn't been anticipated was a language barrier. The *Cambrian Salvor*, often involved in these transfers, had a Dutch Captain and a Japanese crew. On one of these occasions the Senhouse didn't slip. Unaware of the problem, unable to communicate, the *Cambrian Salvor* was pulling the Liberty ships almost on top of the hapless tug behind. Only the quick thinking of the second engineer wielding a cutting torch extricated them.

This was only one of many incidents caused by a lack of communication. One Dutch captain, in a frenzy of irritation and frustration, fired off his rifle in order to get some action out of the crew. Whether this remedy made his message any clearer is debatable but it did get the crew's attention.

There was a reason for the sudden appearance of the Dutch on the horizon.

In 1960 Island Tug had formed a joint venture, Trans Pacific Salvage, with Lendert Smit International, the well-known Dutch firm that was synonymous with the word "salvage." It was a prestigious partner, but the alliance wasn't a one-way street. In fact Island Tug reluctantly introduced Smit to what was, for them, a revolutionary concept.

It happened in mid-Pacific: one of the big Smit tugs with two vessels in tow got her manila towline in her wheel. Another Smit tug and the *Sudbury II* were sent off to split her tow between them. By the time the *Sudbury II* arrived the second Dutch tug had already come and gone with her half of the tow. The *Sudbury II*'s charge, a hulking great aircraft carrier, wallowed gently in the ground swell. There were several Dutch salvage men on her and with their experienced help the crew of the *Sudbury II* got their pennant attached to her and started to let out their towing wire. Slowly they paid it out and slowly the towboat moved farther and farther away from her tow. The Dutchmen had never seen wire towing gear before. At their end it dropped straight into the sea, for none of the slack was taken up at this point. They stared down at the immobile cable that hung from their bows and at the fast-disappearing *Sudbury II*, and thought they were being abandoned. The only English speaker in the group grabbed his walkie-talkie and started shouting at the distant tug. By this time the *Sudbury II* had taken up the slack and was actually towing the carrier. The Dutchman's distress turned to astonishment. He stopped yelling and started asking questions. How long was the towline? he wanted to know. Twenty-six hundred feet, he was told. And what about this wire—did they not use manila line? he asked, and what about the winch? Harley's loyalty was to Island Tug; to him joint ventures meant exactly nothing. "Tell him fuck all," he said, "They're the competition."

On the radio the conversation continued but now it was a long and animated one, in Dutch, between this man and the Smit tug of which only the words "twenty-six hundred feet" were understood by the listeners on the *Sudbury II*. Shortly thereafter the Smit tugs abandoned their huge manila lines and switched to wire.

When these Island Tug vessels eventually returned to their home port from Hawaii and Japan they returned to a company that had reached a crossroads. Island Tug now had a fleet worth $8 million, and it was mortgaged for almost that much. To upgrade this fleet and keep it properly maintained required a large infusion of cash—larger than any financial institution was willing to lend. Harold Elworthy had hit the ceiling that Jim Byrn talks about in Ken Drushka's book *Against Wind and Weather*: "When you're an aggressive independent owner after awhile you reach a ceiling in financing because the industry does not have a large return. You either have to stop growing and consolidate, specialize in one particular portion of the industry, or sell out."

For Harold Elworthy to stop growing or to restrict his business in any other way was unthinkable. From the very start he had stated his aims and business philosophy very clearly: "Surround yourself with good men and continue to expand." Now, in order to practise that philosophy, he would need a vast amount of money. And there were other problems. In 1971, for the first time in the company's history, there was a strike.

Harold Elworthy found it difficult to imagine being confronted by striking employees. Like many self-made men he had assumed the role of patriarch and with it the right to dictate the terms of the employment he provided. During the Depression years and those that followed, jobs were in such short supply that employees accepted this situation because there was little choice. But by the 1950s and '60s they were demanding the autonomy that would permit them to correct some of the very real abuses in the industry. Federal law, for example, provided for adequate rest periods but this law was regularly flouted. "Guys would be towing all night and yarding logs all day," said George Matson. "That's what the strike was all about." Unions, then, had become a fact of life in most of the other towboat companies. H.B., however, remained "virulently anti-union."

"Boys, you don't have to join a union. I'll give you anything you want as long as every other towboat company is doing the same thing," he told his striking employees. But it was the presence of a union that made this bargaining possible and his employees knew it. The picket line around the office remained.

The pickets bore their employer no animosity; each morning both sides exchanged courteous greetings. But the presence of that picket line signalled that Island Tug & Barge could never again be a "family company"; never again would one man dictate the terms of their employment; it would never again be a personal fiefdom, no matter how benevolent. Something had been gained—and something lost. This realization and, more important, the need for larger and larger amounts of financing, convinced Harold Elworthy that the time had come to sell.

All three of H.B.'s sons were in the business now. He himself had become chairman of the board and his eldest son, Arthur, had taken his place as president. Arthur was as astute a businessman as his father, and just as dedicated to the company. Working flat out, he and those around him had achieved great success. The idea of dropping the reins at this point appalled him. "Not yet," he told his father, "not yet. It's too soon to sell." But it was not too soon for H.B.; fifty years of business pressure had taken their toll. Ten years before, he had taken the first step. In October 1960, Sogemine and McAllister Towing, two international companies—one Belgian and one American, respectively—with business ties and ties by marriage, had bought a controlling interest in Island Tug & Barge. The Elworthys had a ten-year contract to supply the operating expertise. Despite Harold Elworthy's assertion that "Island Tug & Barge is still a Canadian company. The control is not outside Canada. I'm still president and my two sons are vice-presidents," it was quite obvious that things *had* changed. Now, in 1970, he sold his remaining shares and Sogemine and McAllister became Island Tug's new owners.

Despite the fact that they were a reputable and highly regarded company, Island Tug's employees were dazed and disturbed. Coming into the office after work, Robbie Robinson, a dispatcher, found the new owners there celebrating their acquisition with champagne.

"Here... have some champagne," someone said, proffering a glass.

For Robbie it wasn't a celebration, it was a wake. He viewed his festive drink and searched for something to say.

"How long are you going to be around?" he finally asked.

"Oh, we're off in the morning."

"That's good," said Robbie. It wasn't a tactful remark; it slipped out before he could censor it. "I didn't mean to be rude," he said, "but what the hell do you say?" What do you say when "your" company has just become "their" company?

Two years later another link to the past was broken. Norman Turner retired and went into business for himself as a marine surveyor. He was a reserved man and he didn't discuss his reason for leaving the company he had served so well for twenty-five years. He had sufficient reason, however, to leave the challenges, the risks, the diversity and the sheer fun of a job he still loved. He was given a generous severance package and a rousing send-off but the newspaper article covering the event made no mention of the debt that Island Tug owed its marine superintendent.

Chapter VIII

The *Offshore 55*

"It was blowing over 90 miles an hour—screaming—huge swells."

By the early 1960s the transpacific towing jobs had dried up. The American government had decided, reasonably enough, that the Japanese shouldn't be profiting from the scrapping of US naval vessels. Tows to the breakup yards of Japan ceased, the partnership with Smit was dissolved and the *Sudbury*s came home.

Now Island Tug had to find other markets for the big tugs' services. They were expensive ships to maintain, so in between more suitable jobs the company hoped they could keep busy with regular coastal work. They sent the *Sudbury II* out with two scows. She was not a powerful tug by today's standards—even then her mate, Jimmy Talbott, said "she couldn't pull the skin off a milk pudding"—yet she was too powerful to tow scows. Any faster than half speed and she pulled them right under the surface of the water. They tried her with a log tow. She went into Cadboro Bay and by the time they had got their heavy towing gear on the boom, it had sunk. Quite obviously these experiments were not successes.

But then, just when it was needed, the *Sudbury*s got a short-term contract to tow barges of chemical liquor back and forth from the pulp mill at Woodfibre in Howe Sound to Gray's Harbor in the US. It was a "non-stop" contract. Come hell or high water they were required to keep the pulp mill supplied. Considering the terms of this contract, it was fortunate that Steve Fairhurst, the *Sudbury*'s captain, had such a cavalier attitude toward bad weather. "We were out in Juan de Fuca Straits," Ray Thomas remembers. "Outside it was blowing over 90 miles an hour—screaming—huge swells. We were doing doughnuts. When I went to bed Steve said, 'We'll head out there. It's going down.' Going down? There were mountains out there."

It was the dead of winter, so these conditions were guaranteed to repeat themselves. In one instance, in a 100-mile-an-hour southeaster, the *Sudbury* was fighting her way past the aptly named Destruction Island. She would go down, bury her whole bow, then struggle up with a load of water and heave it over the pilothouse. Adrian Bull, mate on this voyage, would have liked—indeed, devoutly wished—to slow down but he felt quite sure his captain, the redoubtable Steve, would be critical of any such action, so he persevered. Finally the *Sudbury* dove down and a torrent of water crashed at the wheelhouse with such force that it broke the centre window, left a jagged piece of glass in the quartermaster's arm and embedded the rest of it in the bulkhead behind him. This got Steve's attention. He stormed out of his cabin and raised hell with Adrian for not slowing down. "Of course," said Jim Derby, then the quartermaster, "he would have given him hell if he *had* slowed down."

Like Ed Gait before him, fifteen-year-old Jim Derby had hung around Island Tug pestering everyone for a job. But, unlike Eddie whose parents encouraged him to find work, Jim's parents, and in particular his mother, were determined that he should stay in school. Her son's frequent and unauthorized absences from that institution resulted in several fraught interviews between the principal and Mrs. Derby. Finally the principal offered this advice: "If he can get hired, let him go. He'll be out there for a few months and he'll realize that it's not as glamorous as he imagines. Give him six months. Home will look pretty good to him by then."

No prediction had ever been more wrong. "Our first trip we were out for three months. I would have stayed out there forever," Jim said, "I didn't care if I ever came home. I admired all those guys so much. They were so competent. They had so much to teach me."

Now Jim went to the galley for a dish towel to put around his arm. There was a lot of water sloshing around in the wheelhouse and in the radio room directly behind it. "You better go down below and get a piece of plywood and plug up that window," said the *Sudbury*'s captain to his mate.

In the late summer of 1961 another of the company's tugs relieved the *Sudbury II* on this run while she herself set off for Trinidad towing two barges of machinery that she had picked up in San Francisco. In her engine room George Winterburn was preoccupied with thoughts of alligators. Alligators lived in the tropical countries that they would be visiting and George, an avid hunter, was determined to add one to his collection of trophies. His captain, Harley Blagborne, stuck to the rules much more religiously than John McQuarrie had done, so there were no firearms permitted aboard *his* ship, but George was sure he could find a gun somewhere should the opportunity to use it arise.

George's first chance to track down an alligator occurred when the *Sudbury II* tied up in Colón for a couple of days. He and a shipmate took a bus to the end of the line, where they were elated to find just what they were looking for: a swamp. All day they waded around in the mud without encountering a single alligator. So at the dock the next day George queried the locals, telling them of this failed expedition and seeking their advice on alligator hunting. He got it.

"Man, you're crazy," one of them said, "wading around in a swamp. There's poisonous snakes and you don't know what. You're just lucky you're still around. Swamps are dangerous places."

The *Sudbury II* continued her voyage across the Caribbean to Port of Spain, where she dropped the barges. Wherever she docked, be it in Fukuyama or San Pedro, the routine remained the same. So now, in this busy, dusty, somewhat ramshackle port city, ships' suppliers arrived with meat and fresh produce, the ship was bunkered and her freshwater tanks topped up, the engineers did the work that couldn't be done with the engines running, Harley sat closeted in his cabin doing paperwork and George, not at all deterred by the advice he had received in Colón, went out looking for alligators. This time he avoided swamps and, instead, walked along the banks of a muddy little river. And this time he had better luck: there, dozing in the reeds, lay an alligator. George raced to a nearby farmhouse, knocked on the door and borrowed a gun. He returned to find the alligator still there basking in the sunshine. George shot it—or rather, her, for it turned out to be a female with two foot-long progeny. George now had a problem. He had to transport a very large dead alligator and two vicious baby alligators back to the *Sudbury II.* This entourage was greeted less than enthusiastically by the rest of the crew. Their lack of interest and approval failed to dampen George's spirits, however. He proceeded to skin out the adult alligator and then tucked the hide up in the bows—where the tropical winds soon enveloped the ship in an overpowering stench.

The mate, searching for the source of this asphyxiating smell, came upon George's cache and his instructions were short and to the point: "Throw that goddamn mess over the side," he ordered.

The babies were equally unwelcome, for they proved to be most unsatisfactory pets. "Bite," said George. "You couldn't get near them."

This, of course, wasn't foremost an alligator-hunting trip. Harley got customs clearance, and, the last dockside chore completed, the *Sudbury II* slipped her lines and headed off to the anchorage where her next tow lay waiting. It wasn't hard to find it. The *Offshore 55*, a towering oil rig, was at that time the biggest rig in the world. It was the size and shape of a city block and lay there in the water like a small square island. "And *that's* going to be a bugger to tow," the mate remarked to Harley.

He spoke from experience. George Winterburn reflected on the time they had hooked onto another drilling rig, the *SEDCO.* "We left the VMD with the *SEDCO 135 F* and we just about lost her on the rocks right there. Steve Fairhurst was ringing down 'More power, more power' and we had everything cranked up. It was like hooking onto a rock. It was a horrible thing to tow. The tide had changed and it got a little too strong and we hadn't pulled anything like that before. A Dutch tug came in and picked it up from Esquimalt and took it on down around Race Rocks and headed out Juan de Fuca Strait, and he got outside all right—but then he couldn't move it, so we got a hurry-up call to get out there and give him a hand. He was taking it to New Zealand. It took him forever to get there... months."

The centre of the platform of the *Offshore 55* was filled with drilling equipment and, on either side of this machinery, eight huge jack-up ladders rose a hundred feet in the air. When the rig was in place these ladders became the legs that anchored it to the sea bottom. They could be raised and lowered hydraulically and were now in their raised position; even so, they protruded 10 feet below the waterline and created, the *Sudbury II* crew soon found, enormous drag. "What a lump to tow," said George Winterburn. "Right off the bat Number Four main engine blew up. We had nothing but grief."

Towboat men count patience among their many virtues, however. Day after day, in a flat calm, the *Sudbury II* crawled across the Caribbean and her crew grew to enjoy spending their evenings sitting on the stern under the tropical stars. As they approached the Cayman Islands, however, this idyll came to an abrupt end. Radio reports from the US Weather Service broadcast the warning that a hurricane was brewing several hundred miles astern of them and Harley Blagborne, mindful of the lumbering giant behind him and the four Americans who were riding on it, broadcast his position, course and speed to all stations.

Next day the *Sudbury II*'s radio provided the unsettling news that the hurricane, christened Hattie, was bearing down upon them at increasing speed. Harley altered course to port. The hurricane veered off to port as well. Now there were long slow swells rolling away from the disturbance behind them and a line of ominous black clouds forming. As the wind increased it became capricious, blowing first from one direction and then from another.

Harley talked to the alarmed occupants of the *Offshore 55*, the weather worsening as he spoke. The Americans, having heard those same weather reports, were by now clamouring to be taken off. Harley outlined his plan of action: he would haul in the towline and when the *Sudbury II* was close enough he would launch a life raft and let it drift back to them on a line. "Right at this crucial moment our towing winch loused up," said George Winterburn. "It was an electric winch and it burnt out some wiring. We couldn't retrieve the towline. We cut it." Two thousand feet of wire dropped into the sea.

Harley circled the rig cautiously and brought his stern up as close as he dared. Waves were now breaking over both the tug and the oil rig. Splashing around in this water, the *Sudbury II*'s deck crew launched the life raft and attempted to guide it to its destination. Time after time it slipped past the rig, out of reach of the four life-jacketed figures that clung to the pipe rail there. Then, as those on the *Sudbury II* watched helplessly, a wave burst over the *Offshore 55* and smashed one of the waiting men against the deckhouse. The rig's formidable bulk was now heaving out of the seas, now buried in them. Her jack-up ladders were rattling and shaking with a noise like garbage day in a can factory, broken pipes and machinery clattering across her decks adding to the din. Four times the size of the tug and completely out of control, the rig lurched toward the *Sudbury II* like a menacing drunk. Harley moved the telegraph from Slow Ahead to Half Ahead. From the engine room there was instant compliance. Then the tug's captain picked up the radio-phone that connected him with the oil rig. "How are you guys making out?" His voice was even. Not so the voice that replied.

"For Christ's sake forget that Jeezly life raft and get us off here," it screamed. "Come alongside and get us off. We've got a guy here who's hurt."

"I can't get alongside. That thing would smash us to pieces. I'm going to shoot you a line. It'll be coming against the wind so be ready to grab it quick. Fasten it onto that Carley float you've got and then put the Carley's line around your bollard."

Once more Harley positioned his ship in the heaving seas. From the *Sudbury II*'s stern a line arced through the air and, with

Hit by an approaching hurricane, the Offshore 55 *heaves out of the sea, 1961.* Seaspan

more good luck than good management, landed right at the feet of the men at the rail of the rig. A deckhand bent a heavier line onto it. Now, as Harley had instructed, the raft was secured by two lines—one from the tug, the other from the rig. Fighting for balance, the oil men manhandled their Carley float into the sea and those on the tug's afterdeck hauled in their line. As they pulled it across the 100 feet that separated the two vessels, the waves dropped the raft deep into the troughs and then hurled it into the air.

Reg Caldwell sets out to rescue the Offshore 55*'s crew.* Photo courtesy Jacques Heyrman, Seaspan

The *Sudbury II*'s chief officer, a young Maritimer named Reg Caldwell, now prepared to ride the raft back to the rig. Balanced on the bulwarks, he timed his exit with exquisite precision: as it flew past him on its upward trajectory he scrambled into it and positioned himself carefully in its centre. Now it was the oil men's turn to pull the raft through the waves. They had secured a lifeline to the injured man and as the raft reached the rig and rose on the crest of a wave, the men threw the coil of the line to Reg. The injured man worked his way onto an exposed section of the deck and then, as a wave washed over it, he let go and went with it. Reg reeled him in until he lay sprawled half in and half out of the raft. Shock and pain made any further effort on his part impossible and Reg, fearing that any attempt to wrestle him into the little raft might capsize it, left him there for the few minutes it took them to reach the tug. One by one the others made the perilous journey and clambered over the bulwarks and into the outstretched arms of those on the stern of the tug. Finally Reg, who had supervised their evacuation from the rig, let go the line there and pulled himself across to the tug. Both he and the Carley float were yanked aboard the *Sudbury II*. The little raft remained a souvenir of that day. "We had that Carley around for a long time," Bob Gray remembers.

All contact with the *Offshore 55* had now been severed and, as the tug got clear, those on deck saw the rig drift away and disappear in the maelstrom that surrounded them.

In preparation for her confrontation with Hurricane Hattie, the crew had sealed the *Sudbury II* up as tight as a drum. Now she put her nose to the weather and hove to. Outside her windows there was no sky, no horizon, no sea—just a welter of white that beat down upon her hour after hour. Filled with clutter, the radar screen gave no indication of the whereabouts of the rig. "I just hope we don't run into the bloody thing," said Harley.

For twenty-four hours the *Sudbury II* strained upwards, shuddered and then slid down into yawning troughs. Roaring down her decks, the seas momentarily buried her. Over and over again she shook off her load of water and prepared to do battle with the next wave. Not for the first time, those on the *Sudbury II* marvelled at the extraordinary sea-keeping qualities of their ship as she faced down this Caribbean hurricane with implacable resolve. Finally Hurricane Hattie tired of the contest and turned westward to vent its fury on British Honduras.

The ship that emerged from this hurricane looked like the survivor of a war, which, in a way, she was. Seawater slammed through the air by Force 12 winds had beaten great patches of paint not only from her hull and her superstructure, but from her mast. From the bridge the deck officer stared up in bemusement at crosstrees that had been "power washed" right down to their bare metal. Visibility restored, all eyes searched the horizon and the radar for whatever was left of the *Offshore 55*.

"If that thing is still afloat, I'll be the most surprised guy on this ship," said the mate and Harley was inclined to agree. Still, in the confused seas that followed the storm, they began a criss-cross search pattern. For a day and a night they combed the sea for a large object that was probably on the bottom. And then, early one morning, a Coast Guard aircraft got them on the radio. "Found your missing oil rig," they announced cheerily. "It's on San Pedro Reef, off British Honduras."

The *Sudbury II* went off to investigate. In the three days it had been on its own, the *Offshore 55* had drifted some 500 miles before it fetched up on the reef. It had come in on a big sea and dropped down, embedding itself in the coral. On the bottom of each of its jack-up ladders there was a doughnut-shaped pad 20 feet in diameter. On the seaward side the rig was floating but on the landward side these ladders had driven themselves 10 feet into the coral. The *Offshore 55*, its waterlogged bulk at a drunken angle, was well and truly impaled. The *Sudbury II* headed for New Orleans for divers, equipment and an assist tug.

It was an American salvage man on the assist tug who came up with a salvage plan. Perhaps, based as he was in the Gulf of Texas, he had had more experience with coral reefs. In any case it was not a particularly sophisticated plan. "We'll just hook the towlines on her and start pulling," he said. So they pumped the seawater out of the rig and then hooked up the towlines. The two tugs, "just all cranked up and pulling like a son-of-a-gun," kept at it while divers dug away at the coral with pressure hoses. The trade winds helped, creating a constant swell that rocked the floating end and worked the buried legs. Still, for the first couple of weeks there was no discernible movement. The crew, sitting on the stern in the sunshine, could look down at the sea bottom and see the same conch shells that they'd seen days before; the rig hadn't moved an inch. As the bottom shelved off, however, the rig came faster and faster and finally it came clear—twenty-seven days after they began.

CHAPTER IX

The *Glafkos* and Other Voyages

"I just about died on the spot."

In the first week of 1962, while the *Sudbury II* was still on her way home from the Caribbean, the Greek ship *Glafkos* ran aground on the west coast of Vancouver Island, and the SS *Sudbury* and her crew were introduced to some intrepid citizens of Ucluelet and to a skillful and daring helicopter pilot.

In Ucluelet the first intimation of trouble came in the early evening of New Year's Day, when George Hillier, a fisherman and the local search and rescue coordinator, arrived at his neighbour's house to use the telephone.

"Want to borrow your phone, Ray. There's somebody in trouble out there."

Ray Vose and his wife lived right on the waterfront. Over George's shoulder Ray saw distress flares arcing into the darkness, as if to confirm George's words.

Ray was a ham radio operator. He switched on his set and found the distress channel rattling with urgent conversation. Minutes later George Hillier was involved in that conversation and soon after that his seiner, the *Hillier Queen*, was backing out of her mooring and turning toward the entrance of the bay. It had been a quiet, drizzly west coast day but late in the afternoon a strong southeaster got up and it was now shaking the Voses' house.

As rocket after rocket shot up over the open sea the whole village of Ucluelet became aware that a drama was taking place somewhere out there in the dark. Ray's next visitor was his friend, Jim Hill. The two men sat rivetted to the conversation on the distress band. George Hillier, it appeared, was as near as he dared get to the stricken vessel, which was identified as the Greek ship *Glafkos*. She was impaled on a rock, which had penetrated her engine room, and she was being pounded by the southeaster. Without power she was using her short-range emergency transmitter to communicate. They listened to George describe the situation to Search and Rescue: "I can't get alongside. There's a big sea out here and she's got rocks all around her. The only way I can get anyone off is with a breeches buoy. We could use the halibut ground line but I haven't got it with me."

Jim Hill had fished on the *Hillier Queen*. "I know where that ground line is," he told Ray. "In the gear shed across the bay. We could get it and take it out to him in your boat."

Ray's boat was a 14-foot outboard. Out past the entrance to the bay, the winds were gusting at over 40 miles an hour and the waves were 20 feet high. Ucluelet, on the wild west coast of Vancouver Island, is not the place to live unless you are "good on the water." Both these men were. There was no hesitation. They struggled into oilskin jackets, lit a couple of lanterns and climbed into the boat, which was moored at the float in front of Ray's house. They crossed the bay, retrieved the pile of ground line and headed out into the open sea. Now the full force of the wind hit their small boat. "She was a good little boat," said Ray, "and I had a brand new outboard. Otherwise I don't think I'd have tried it."

Ahead they could see the *Hillier Queen* rearing and plunging in the bright pool of light from the floodlights on her afterdeck. Concentrating on holding his position, George didn't notice the approaching outboard. When he did, he was dumbfounded.

"What in hell are you guys doing out here?"

"Brought your ground line," yelled Jim.

Somehow they heaved it onto the deck of the seiner.

"Well, since you're here," shouted George, "maybe you can get out to the freighter and find out what's going on."

The men in the little boat waved and headed out into the darkness. The two hand lanterns that served as their running lights marked their erratic progress. The *Glafkos* was imprisoned by what the newspapers later described as a "nest of rocks" and each of these was white with breaking waves.

"We went over through the breakers," said Ray, "and found the crew all hanging over the rail. They didn't speak English so we didn't get very far. A huge swell was running down the side of the ship so I was pretty busy trying to keep the boat heading into it. But then somebody lowered an empty wine bottle with a message in it."

They took it back to the *Hillier Queen*. It was a message from the freighter's captain, asking them to contact the vessel's agent.

"I don't think she's going to sink on us and I can't do a damned thing till daylight," said George. "Just go in and pass along the message to the shipping agent."

By this time the tug *Island Challenger* had joined the *Hillier Queen* and the lighthouse keeper at Amphitrite Point had notified the Bamfield lifeboat station. The lifeboat snatched up the three men who were available and by 10:00 p.m. they had fought their way through the gale-force winds and were there as well. In the lashing rain and sleet that had now started to fall, this little flotilla stood by. On their radio-telephones they expressed the fervent hope that if the *Glafkos* did break up she would wait for daylight to do so. That way they would have some chance of picking up her crew members.

"It was lucky the *Glafkos* people dropped their hooks right away," said Bill Fullerton, the coxswain on the lifeboat. "If they hadn't, I think her stern would have swung onto Jenny Reef and if that had happened she would have been a goner."

By now more help was on its way. Within hours of the *Glafkos*'s grounding, the *Sudbury* was ready to go to her aid; at twenty minutes past midnight she pulled away from the Island Tug dock in Victoria and by 10:00 the next morning she was rolling around in a southeast gale off Amphitrite Point. Her captain, Steve Fairhurst, sized up the situation: the *Glafkos* straddled a reef with another, Jenny Reef, just north of her. She was surrounded by rocks. Neither the *Sudbury* nor the *Challenger* could get near her. While the two tug captains discussed their nonexistent options on their radios, the seas, growing higher as the wind rose, washed the *Glafkos* off the reef and fetched her up on her anchors some 50 feet from Jenny Reef. This was not an entirely unsatisfactory development; her bow, at least, was clear of the breakers.

Steve got on the radio to the Bamfield lifeboat. "Can you go in and sound around the bow?"

Within minutes they reported good water from midships to bow on the starboard side.

Steve took the *Sudbury* in. On her afterdeck the mate readied the rocket gun. The wind had reached 45 miles per hour. Over and over again it blew the rocket's light line away from its target but finally, some two and a half hours after their first attempt, the deck crew had a towline secured to the *Glafkos*. Steve took up the slack and worked up to Full Ahead. Water churning out astern, the *Sudbury* managed to drag the freighter some 900 feet, and then the line parted. The *Glafkos* settled back on her anchors 300 feet from Jenny Reef.

Now it was the *Challenger*'s turn: drawing less than the *Sudbury*, she was the obvious choice. Her captain, "Mickey" McPherson, took her in, picking his way around breaking rocks. Up close to the Greek, fighting to hold his position in the seas, Mickey ordered his line fired. After a few failed attempts the *Challenger* finally got coupled up to the freighter's bow. The wind had risen to 55 miles per hour and the seas had grown ever more ferocious. There was no hope of transferring the towing pennant to the *Sudbury* so the smaller tug hung on, holding her charge away from the rocks all Tuesday night. By early Wednesday morning this continuous effort was beginning to tell on both her engine and her captain. Mickey McPherson had been in the wheelhouse for more than thirty hours by now, his meals brought to him by the mate. It was not a regime calculated to improve the health of a man with a heart condition.

At daylight on January 3 the wind had moderated enough to transfer the towing pennant to the *Sudbury*, and the *Challenger*

The Sudbury *and the grounded Greek ship* Glafkos, *1962. The anchors that had saved the* Glafkos *by keeping her off the reef now prevented her rescue—the* Sudbury *couldn't move her with her anchors holding fast.*
Ryan Bros. photo, Seaspan

made for Ucluelet for engine repairs and a brief respite for her captain. But now the anchors that had saved the *Glafkos* prevented her rescue: the *Sudbury* couldn't move her with her anchors still holding fast. Steve contacted Tofino radio with instructions to radio the *Glafkos* and tell her captain to let go his anchor chains. Minutes passed. The *Glafkos*'s starboard anchor chain rattled out of its hawse pipe but at that point her captain seemed to have had second thoughts. He informed Tofino that he wasn't prepared to let go the port anchor until there were two tugs holding him. The wind had increased once again and huge seas pounded the Greek now; her single anchor was dragging and her stern was swinging toward George Fraser Islands. Steve slammed the telegraph handle back and forth and left it with its indicator pointing an accusatory finger at the words "Full

Ahead." In the engine room the Chief, correctly assuming some crisis, gave him everything he had. Then, in an all-out effort to hold her position, the *Sudbury* dropped her own anchor.

Meanwhile those on the *Glafkos* decided that their time had come. Expecting their ship to break up momentarily, they made a desperate bid for their lives. The inhabitants of Ucluelet, lining the shore, watched them attempt to lower a lifeboat. It hit the water and smashed itself against the side of the ship. Waterlogged, it continued to crash against the *Glafkos* with every sea until it tore its rigging loose and drifted away.

And then, shortly after noon, there was the reverberating clatter of an approaching helicopter and the RCAF's giant twin-rotor rescue craft swept in over the treetops and hovered low over the stern of the *Glafkos*. Carefully it moved in till it was a scant 50 feet above the tiny figures crouched below. Then crew members lowered a sling, and one by one they winched six crewmen into the craft's belly. Now it banked steeply, its rotors thudding, and disappeared. Ten minutes later it was back to repeat the process until all who remained on the *Glafkos* were her master, three officers and a fireman.

As long as the *Glafkos*'s anchor held, Steve Fairhurst felt he had no hope of saving her and the Greek captain remained adamantly opposed to dropping his remaining anchor chain. The *Sudbury*, however, was not to be deterred. She had never lost a ship and she was not about to break that record now. Roy Blake got on the radio-telephone to a machine shop in Ucluelet. The conversation was brisk and to the point.

"Have you got any welding equipment there?"

"Yeah, we've got an acetylene outfit."

"Have you got a couple of welders?"

"Well, yeah. Pete Hillier and Malcolm Miller can weld."

"Would they take their welding equipment and drop down from the helicopter onto the *Glafkos*?"

Long pause. "Yes."

So, shortly before high tide, Pete Hillier and Malcolm Miller, their welding equipment, 700 feet of nylon towline and a cheap walkie-talkie were loaded into the big Sikorsky, and this "flying banana" clattered up and over the roiling sea.

Just when the Glafkos*'s crew thought the ship would break up under them, an RCAF rescue helicopter swept in over the treetops and hovered low over the stern.* Photo courtesy Beverly Bruce

Malcolm was not a particularly happy camper. As an air force winchman proceeded to fasten him into a canvas harness, Malcolm tried to get a feel for the crew's expertise.

"Do you do a lot of this kind of thing?" he asked.

"Well, we were out on a forest fire job a week ago," the airman said. "We pulled a lot of guys out of that." There was a pause. "The last guy didn't make it. The cable broke."

And I am sorry I asked, thought Malcolm.

The airman now slid back a door on the side of the aircraft and a 40-knot wind came blasting into the cabin, buffeting its occupants. The crewman gestured for Malcolm to sit on the floor in the open doorway. With some reluctance he complied, his feet now dangling in space. Below him the *Glafkos* looked "about 2 inches long." As he tried to come to terms with this dizzying spectacle, he found himself, quite without warning, hanging in mid-air. Now sheer terror washed over him. "I just about died on the spot," he said. He remained practical, however. If I pass out, I'll slip right out of this harness, he told himself. With enormous effort he dragged his eyes away from his bird's-eye view and concentrated instead on his fingernails! All the way down to the *Glafkos*'s deck he examined his nails intently.

The huge waves that were pounding the *Glafkos* heaved her skyward and then dropped her. Her decks rose and fell with the speed of an elevator. The watchers on shore, including Ray Vose, were now witness to a remarkable example of co-ordination. Hovering over the freighter's deck, the pilot synchronized the ship's movement with his own in order to minimize the shock for those landing on the deck. "That pilot should have had a medal," Ray said.

"All very well for him to say," said Malcolm. "He wasn't there." Malcolm was. He dropped onto the deck and fumbled frantically with the harness's fastenings. Before he could extricate himself he was once more hoisted high into the air as the *Glafkos* dropped away into the trough. In desperate haste he snapped the fastenings shut again. His second landing provided enough time for him to get clear of the harness.

Now Pete was winched down. Malcolm yanked him out of his harness and the two of them landed the welding equipment and the towline. They found five remaining members of the *Glafkos*'s crew on board: the captain, a couple of mates, the wireless operator and a fireman who had been so drunk he passed out and missed his chance to be rescued by the helicopter. "The fireman," Malcolm said, "was quite obviously in the captain's bad books. He was trying to make amends, rushing around trying to find some hot water so the captain could shave." The captain, for his part, made it clear that he wanted nothing to do with either Pete or Malcolm and he locked himself in his cabin; the others were not much more helpful.

The wind had dropped once again. The *Sudbury*, pulling with all the power she could muster, was now dragging the *Glafkos* and her anchor toward the Caroline Channel buoy. Something had to give; fortunately it was the anchor chain and not the towline. Before Malcolm and Pete could attack it with their torch, it snapped. But in order to keep the suddenly freed freighter off the shore, the tug was now pulling so hard that her captain feared the towline would be next. So Malcolm and Pete, following his radioed instructions, concentrated on getting a second line connected to the *Challenger*, now back in the fray once again. They dragged their 3-inch line to the bow, secured it to a tow bit and pulled the rest of it down the length of the ship, dropping it overboard as they went. At this point they discovered to their distress that it didn't float, but sank. So the two men started all over again. Laboriously they hauled in the wet line and followed another procedure. They dragged the line the length of the ship, fastening it to the rails as they went, and then hung the remainder from the ship's fantail. Now it fell to Mickey McPherson to thread his way through the rocks once again and pick up the line from the *Glafkos*'s stern.

"When she heaves up, I'm going right in under her counter," he yelled at the three deckhands clustered at the bow. "You've got three seconds."

Buffeted by the wind, the *Challenger* waited for her moment. The freighter's looming stern started upward. The tug swept in, the deckhands grabbed the line and took a turn on a cleat, and the *Challenger* went full astern. Above, Pete and Malcolm rushed to unfasten the line along the freighter's side.

By now it was dark. Against considerable odds and without her captain's blessing, the water-filled *Glafkos* was under tow and on her way to Victoria. So were Pete Hillier and Malcolm Miller. And, they reflected, there were better forms of transportation. The ship was dark and very cold; two of her holds and her engine room were full of water and there was still a sea running. Every time she rolled, "all the stuff inside her would start banging and crashing around." It would have been an unnerving experience for anyone, let alone the two non-seamen. Malcolm remembered reading about ships like this that broke in half and the two tried to decide which half of the *Glafkos* would be more likely to stay afloat in this event. Every half hour the *Sudbury* called them on their walkie-talkie, the batteries of which were fading fast. And a lot can happen in half an hour, Malcolm told himself.

To distract themselves from their plight the two men took their flashlights and made a tour of the ship. They found that the deck above the crew's quarters was so rusted that water dripped down onto the bunks below. In the galley the provisions were securely locked in slatted compartments under the floor. In the pilothouse there was a compass but no other navigational equipment. There were two pairs of binoculars there and Pete and Malcolm considered taking them as souvenirs. "When we discovered they were about four power, we gave up the idea," said Malcolm.

Steve Fairhurst's log read:

> January 4, 1962 02:00 hours abeam Tatoosh Island,
> weather calm, towing gear reported in fine shape from
> the S.S. Glafkos
> 08:00 abeam Race Rocks
> 09:30 picked up Pilot
> 11:30 hours S.S. Glafkos moored to drydock wall at
> Esquimalt Harbour.

"We got day wages and bus fare home," said Malcolm, "and the company gave us a real good breakfast in the Princess Mary restaurant."

The rescue of the *Glafkos* left several intriguing questions unanswered. Her captain was quoted as saying that he was heading for the Strait of Juan de Fuca and that he was "off course." The Strait of Juan de Fuca lies some 100 miles to the south of Ucluelet. Given his virtually nonexistent navigational aids, however, this could have been the case. Yet he also explained that he had run aground in heavy fog and that no foghorn was sounding. The lighthouse keeper at Amphitrite Point said that there was no fog and that he could see the ship 3 miles offshore. Les Rimes, reporting the incident for the *Vancouver Sun*, was struck by the fact that although the ship's hull was punctured, no bunker oil fouled the beaches. Was it possible that, like some before her, the *Glafkos* had sold fuel to an unknown party—rather more fuel than she should have—and that she was descending upon the startled village of Ucluelet in the hope of buying enough to take her to her destination?

The *Sudbury II* arrived back in Victoria on January 17, 1962, and joined her namesake on the mundane job that became known as the Rock Run. She left Victoria, towing an empty barge, in time to be at Blubber Bay at 8:00 a.m. Monday morning. By 11:00 that night the barge was loaded with 11 1/2 thousand tons of limestone; tug and tow then departed for Astoria, on the Columbia River. The men who had navigated the Inland Sea of Japan, passed in and out of San Francisco and Honolulu, and followed the Great Circle Route that skirted the Aleutians and the northeastern tip of Russia, now grappled with a new challenge: the Columbia River Bar.

The great Columbia River, pouring out of the Canadian Rockies, ends its journey to the sea on the Oregon coast, the silt and sand it brings with it forming a vast bar at the river's mouth. Here wind, current and shallow water create one of the most treacherous stretches of water on the west coast. The strong ebb of the river running against the constant swell of the Pacific produces short, sharp seas capable of lifting up a ship and slamming her onto the bottom, thus "breaking her back."

To prevent this unfortunate occurrence the bar is closed to marine traffic when the waves are higher than 14 feet. So now the *Sudbury*s, on regular runs from Blubber Bay to Astoria, had to negotiate the bar and the confines of the river when weather permitted and, worse still, had to stay outside when gales closed the bar. They could be out there for days, going dead slow, making the great gradual turns which took them from Tillamook Head in the south to the Lightship in the north. On those days seas chest-high swept over the *Sudbury*s. George Matson remembers going aft to change the nip in the towline. As he came around the housework on his return, a towering wave stared him full in the face. “Jeeesus Christ,” he breathed to no one in particular.

In the beginning there was no pilotage at the river’s entrance, but a pilot soon became compulsory. Both John Watt and George Matson agreed that they preferred it without the pilot because, as George said, “In the first place pilots don’t know one thing about towing and then, of course, it’s a bit hair-raising trying to board a pilot out there because it gets pretty rough and they come along in a small boat. My heart used to be in my mouth sometimes.” And, periodically, pilots *were* lost.

Even in good weather, crossing the bar with that huge bargeload of limestone presented a challenge. The tug shortened up her towline and one and a half hours after low water she made her entrance. The timing of this entrance was critical. She couldn’t run at full speed because of the short towline, yet she had to have enough power to buck the outflow of the river. The mate stood by the winch, which was on a soft brake, and each time the bar’s breakers dragged towing wire astern the mate recovered as much of it as possible. “It was a beautiful winch. You could play the barge like a fish,” said John Watt. There was a telegraph back aft by the winch and John, caught up in the business of reeling in the barge, would forget, use it like a wheelhouse control and then wonder why the engine’s response was so slow. He’d wonder, that is, until the Chief appeared. “For God’s sake *ring* the damned thing,” he would roar.

Ray Thomas and the Chief, Harry Sapro, had an even more spirited exchange.

“I went back to shorten the towline and I told Harry I wouldn’t need the telegraph controls at the stern. We started to shorten up and all of a sudden the line let go and started to run out! I’m doing about a third ahead, just slow, but I couldn’t stop her—I had no controls. I phoned the engine room and yelled, ‘Harry, there’s something gone wrong with the winch; it's running out. Give me the controls back here and do something with the winch.'

"'There's nothing wrong with the winch.'

"'Well, give me the controls here.'

"I stopped the boat and then put her astern to take the weight off the towline. Everything stopped. We had about 50 feet of towline left.

"Harry came up. We were both furious. We were ready to tear each other's heads off. He was mad because he figured I didn't know what I was doing. I figured that it was his fault because he wasn't paying attention to the electrical system. We were set to throw each other over the side. The Romanians weren't the first ones to feel like throwing someone overboard."

One would think that once in the flat waters of the Columbia River their troubles would be over, but not so. The temperamental Cooper-Bessemers were now the problem. They would leave Blubber Bay with all four running but by the time they reached the US they would have suffered through any number of combinations and permutations: at various times they would have one, three, four or two engines running. This was bad enough in the open sea. In the confines of the Columbia River it was hair-raising.

John Watt remembers coming up the river.

"I've got to knock an engine off," said the engine room.

Minutes later they were back. "I've got to knock off another engine."

They were now down to two and they needed one for deck power. They were approaching the Astoria dock to put off the pilot.

"There was no backup," John remembers. He tried Full Astern and then he tried Flank. There was no appreciable response. Various religious words flitted through his mind. The tug's captain and the pilot exchanged glances. "What can you do?" said John.

The *Sudbury II* sailed blithely ahead. There was a jarring collision and then the disconcerting sound of splintering timbers. Fifteen feet into the wharf, the *Sudbury II* finally stopped.

Such were the joys of the Rock Run.

CHAPTER X

The *Lefkipos*

"Nylon . . . nylon."

Emergencies demand a swift response, and everyone at Island Tug understood this. Even the company's insurance broker was not surprised to get a call in the middle of the night. This was actually the preferred time to make such calls, as far as the Island Tug dispatcher was concerned. Charged with calling the crew, he knew where to find them at that hour—at home in bed. The second-best time and place to get the crew together in a hurry was at the Christmas party. Celebrants who saw Robbie Robinson striding purposefully toward them knew that for them, the party was over.

Even in the daylight hours, however, the dispatcher tracked his quarry with the relentless determination of a bloodhound. "They could give you fourteen bloody reasons why they couldn't go," he said, "but they always did go."

Bob Gray's experience was typical. "I remember we were Christmas shopping in Woodward's," he said. "The next thing you know they were paging us on the public-address system. Even if you were due some time off, you went when they called. You knew they needed you."

At a time like New Year's Eve it was especially hard to get a crew together at short notice. Pete Van de Putte, who lived in Vancouver, was once called on the last day of the year.

"Oh I'm so glad I got you," said Vicky from the office. "I've got Scottie Miller on standby. He will take a taxi to your house and pick you up and you two will proceed to the airport. We already have two seats bumped on Flight 14; you won't have to go near the ticket counter, just straight on the plane. They're holding it for you."

Pete wished his wife and infant daughter a happy new year and was gone.

Racing into Victoria from the airport, their taxi was broadsided by another car. This contretemps upset the driver considerably; his passengers, however, were too single-minded to be sympathetic.

"Never mind the goddamned taxi," they bellowed at the poor man. "Get on the radio and get us some wheels."

Nor did you have to be a regular crew member to be snatched away at a moment's notice. Ed Creed was a shore engineer. When his phone rang at 2:00 a.m. it was Norman Turner at the other end.

"Can you come down to work for a little while, Ed? There's been an accident up off Nanaimo and we need a hand to load some gear."

Ed loaded gear. Trucks loaded with provisions rolled onto the dock and discharged them. The *Sudbury II* was set to go.

"Hop aboard, Ed," said Turner. "I'll phone your wife."

It was three weeks before he got home.

Experienced people with the right tickets were in short supply and this created a problem for the dispatchers and tested their powers of persuasion. Short one licensed mate for the *Sudbury*, Robbie Robinson phoned Captain Kirkendale, who ran one of the little harbour tugs.

"Ah, um . . . aw no," said this gentleman.

"Now Dave, we're really pressed. We wouldn't bother you if we didn't have to."

"But Robbie," wailed the reluctant Captain Kirkendale, "we just got a TV."

Despite all these very human problems the *Sudbury*s' departures were swiftly and efficiently organized. Much practice had seen to that; suppliers opened shop at any hour of the day or night, planes were held, insurance was written, crew members were snatched up. In the case of the *Lefkipos*, only a few miles off the coast of Vancouver Island, this was fortuitous. There was not a lot of time to spare.

On March 12, 1966, the agents for the 4,900-ton Greek vessel *Lefkipos* contacted Island Tug to tell them that she was disabled some 70 miles off Cape Flattery and was drifting toward the reef-strewn west coast of Vancouver Island. The call was received at 11:00 a.m. and by 1:00 p.m. the *Sudbury II* had cleared Victoria Harbour and was proceeding at full speed toward the position given by the Greek.

By 9:00 that same night the *Sudbury II* had made radio-telephone contact with the *Lefkipos*, which now supplied a new position. Since 11:00 that morning she had drifted 30 miles. She also delivered the less than cheering news that she had no power on deck and would not be able to stop off an anchor in order to make the anchor cable available to shackle the towline.

The *Sudbury II* had left Victoria in moderate easterly winds. By the time she reached the *Lefkipos* at 1:45 the following morning, there was a gale blowing. Even worse, the Greek ship had drifted to within 8 miles of Bajo Reef. Steve Fairhurst, the *Sudbury II*'s captain on this trip, had spent twenty of his forty-one years at sea in this area of the coast, and as they neared their quarry he made some calculations. He estimated that the *Lefkipos*'s rate of drift up to the time of their arrival had been approximately 3 knots. That rate would most certainly have accelerated in the howling winds that were now buffeting both ships. His experience in the area told him that the line of drift would be northward, closing the coast, and he estimated that in a maximum time of six hours the M/S *Lefkipos* would be in a very hazardous position, prone to be driven ashore on the reefs in the area adjacent to Tatchu Point, with total loss almost a certainty.

Steve decided that the quickest way to bring the Greek ship under control was to put a manila line on her. He could then proceed to the more sheltered waters of Nootka Sound, where they could switch to towing wire. So the deck crew dragged 1,000 feet of 10-inch manila line out of the hold and coiled it on deck.

It was dark, there were gale-force winds and heavy seas, and time was of the essence for they were closing in on a reef. Steve manoeuvred his vessel into position under the bow of the *Lefkipos*—so close that a heaving line could be thrown down from the foredeck of the Greek. The *Sudbury*'s deckhands bent an inch-and-a-half polypropylene line onto this as an intermediate step before sending up the towline itself. As they did this, the Greek crewmen, acutely conscious of the fact that they had no power and would have to haul in the line by hand, leaned over the bulwarks and used one of their few English words.

"Nylon," they exhorted, "nylon."

A good look at the procedure involved in coupling up a tow. A heaving line stretches from the stricken ship to the Sudbury II. *At the stern, two men have attached a poly line. It, in turn, has been fastened to a manila line, which has been attached to the towing wire (foreground).* Sheret photo, Seaspan

When they pulled in the *Sudbury II*'s inch-and-a-half poly they thought their prayers had been answered. They were considerably downcast when the tug's deck crew, using animated sign language, made them understand that they must now pull in 300 feet of poly and then a huge manila towline.

The action of the waves had now separated the two ships, leaving a large bight of manila line in the water. The only thing heavier than 10-inch circumference manila is 10-inch circumference manila that is soaking wet. To ease the Greeks' labours Steve Fairhurst got the *Sudbury II*'s stern into position and then, with exquisite precision, held her just far enough away from the freighter to keep the line out of the water—in weather his log records as "Southeast gale. Rough sea." Steve Fairhurst was a short man, "not a lot taller than the telegraph," but as Jim Derby said, "He was one of the best there ever was. He had good judgment and lots of guts. I've seen him do stuff that nobody else could ever do." Now, for two hours, while the *Lefkipos*'s deck crew dragged in the 10-inch towline manually and made it fast, he held the tug there. The *Sudbury II*'s first mate, eyes glued to the radar, periodically reported the positions of the two vessels in relation to the rocky shoreline. At 3:45 a.m. the manila towline was secure and the *Sudbury II* began to pull her charge away from the rocks.

By next morning the weather had eased but, even towing at reduced speed, the manila hawser chafed itself apart at the *Lefkipos*'s bow. Off Estevan Point the *Sudbury II* hauled in the broken towline and once again manoeuvred into position under the bow of the Greek, whose crew pulled in towing wire this time and secured it; then at Nootka Sound some of the *Sudbury II*'s deck crew clambered aboard the *Lefkipos* and, using the tug's winch, hoisted up some lengths of towing chain, which was used as a bridle and connected to the towing wire.

By 8:00 a.m. on March 15 the *Sudbury II* had delivered her charge to Vancouver. There, for the first time, the two captains met and signed Lloyd's Open Form.

The *Sudbury II*, rescuer of the *Lefkipos*, was now the only *Sudbury*. On March 6, 1966, just a week before the *Sudbury II* headed out to rescue the Greek, her sister ship had had some minor repairs done on her after boiler. When the steamfitters left, they told the fireman on board that the job was done and that he could raise steam on the boilers. Steam up, she lay at her moorings in the inner harbour and, it being Saturday evening, her caretaker felt an irresistible urge to head for the nearest beer parlour. This gentleman returned to the ship some hours later considerably sauced and fell into bed without checking the water level in the glass. It dropped, the safety valve blew, the tube plate collapsed and at 2:00 a.m. the boiler exploded. Roused from a deep sleep, the fireman galloped up the dock, his glasses askew, his clothes in disarray, yelling "Fire!"

After considerable buck-passing, report-writing and consultation, the bottom line was quite evident: the damage to the SS *Sudbury* was beyond repair. The ship that had towed so many vessels to safety was now herself towed across the narrow stretch of water to Morris Greene's Capital Iron and Metal, and men with cutting torches descended upon her. In short order she was reduced to piles of hacked-up plating. There was nothing left to mourn. Victoria's *Daily Colonist* carried a long and moving tribute to her, and she disappeared into oblivion. Now there was only *Sudbury II*.

And the *Sudbury II*, herself, faced an uncertain future. Island Tug & Barge had grown by absorbing other companies and now it, in turn, had been absorbed. In 1960 McAllister/Sogemine had bought controlling interest in the company. In 1961 they bought Griffiths Steamship Company and then the remaining shares of Island Tug. It was another step in the life cycle of big business—the large swallowing the small in progressively bigger chunks—and it continued as McAllister/Sogemine took over Vancouver Tug in 1970 and continued its metamorphosis through mergers and name changes to emerge in 1971 as Seaspan.

The infusion of capital that came with this new ownership sparked, among other things, a discussion regarding the future of the *Sudbury II*. She was aging and her Cooper-Bessemers were not aging gracefully. In 1969 Vancouver newspapers published articles outlining the complete refit that was proposed for her. An artist's rendering showed a streamlined and completely renovated ship. Her engines, the articles stated, were to be replaced with two 10,500 hp General Motors.

An artist's sketch depicting the Sudbury II*'s proposed refit, 1969. The refit was not to be.* Colin Bradbury photo, Seaspan

But it was not to be. Arthur Elworthy was disappointed. He still believed that salvage could be a profitable part of the business; over and over he had seen limited exposure reap large rewards. But he was overruled. The indisputable evidence, provided by the company's ledgers, showed that the *Sudbury II* cost more to maintain than she was earning. Liberty ships and aircraft carriers and broken-down Greeks were now in short supply. The market for her services didn't warrant an expensive refit. The *Sudbury II* remained in limbo.

For the Island Tug men the merger with the Vancouver Tugboat Company was an especially painful experience. For years Island Tug and Vancouver Tug had been fierce competitors, and it was not a friendly rivalry. Now, like the blended family of divorce, the employees of the two companies were required to "get along." "Now there was a completely different philosophy of management," said George Hunter. "They played Good Cop, Bad Cop. And for the first time we were required to supply our own binoculars and tools, 'otherwise they'd be stolen'."

Perhaps they would have been; it was a big company now and big companies have to run things differently. But it was a slap in the face for men who had been trusted implicitly.

Those at Island Tug watched, powerless and bitter, as their new and more powerful "siblings" worked diligently to erase all trace of the company they had served so proudly. The office was dismantled, the shipyard sold, the ships renamed. All but two of Island Tug's meticulously prepared salvage reports were sent, not to the Maritime Museum where they belonged as part of Victoria's history, but to the shredder. The black binders with the gold lettering contained charts, log extracts, photos, biographies of the officers involved and hour-by-hour accounts of each salvage job. They were the record of a remarkable company's capabilities and achievements. Now they and that company were gone.

CHAPTER XI

The *Mandoil II*

"Mother of God, save us all."

Effectively isolated from the visible world by the early darkness of a winter afternoon and a dense fog, dimly lit by the small glow of the binnacle and the twinkling lights of the electronic equipment, the pilothouse of the steam tanker *Mandoil II* seemed suspended in space. Ten years old, the 700-foot *Mandoil II* was a state-of-the-art example of Dutch shipbuilding expertise. Now, on the last day of February 1968, she thrummed along some 340 miles off the mouth of the Columbia River, carrying 300,000 barrels of light Sumatra crude oil. For a few moments her mate watched wisps of fog stream by the windows. Then he turned his attention to the radar screen and as the sweeping electronic line illuminated blips he went rigid with horror. Even as he stared at the screen another ship burst through the wall of fog and tore into the starboard bow of his own ship. There was the ear-splitting screech of tearing metal and a shower of sparks fanned into the air. Instantly a great fireball erupted and rolled down the length of the vessel, destroying everything in its path. On the other ship, a log carrier, the deck cargo burst into flames. Then the groundswell worked the ships apart, and within minutes each was drifting alone in the fog.

The tanker was blazing from stem to stern and settling in the water. Her radio was silent. But from the log carrier a voice, taut with terror, screamed into the radio, "Mayday, Mayday, Mayday... Mayday."

San Francisco Coast Guard radio picked up the message and tried, without success, to get a word in edgewise.

Hysterical from the carnage that surrounded it, the voice continued to yell "Mayday" until it ran out of breath. Only then could San Francisco get the vessel's name and position. She was the Japanese ship *Suwaharu Maru* and she gave her position as latitude 46°6 N, longitude 132°18 W.

The radio officers on half a dozen nearby ships picked up her distress call and the *Kure Maru*, the closest to the scene of the collision, changed course and headed for the given position. Then a US Coast Guard plane rumbled out of the murk and circled over the area, its lights appearing and disappearing in the banks of fog.

The tanker, great gusts of fire billowing out of her, presented a spectacular sight. Guided by the glaring light of flames that could be seen 10 miles away, the *Kure Maru* arrived and launched her boats. They crisscrossed the water looking for bobbing heads and picked thirty-three shell-shocked survivors out of the sea, including the badly burned captain, Elia Karavitis.

The *Suwaharu Maru* had identified herself but the *Mandoil II*'s identity was unknown until these water-soaked crewmen supplied the name of their vessel. The information was relayed to the Coast Guard in San Francisco, and there the vessel's name was searched out in a shipping registry and her agent notified of the disaster. Shortly thereafter, two ship owners, one Japanese and one Greek, received the unwelcome news that their ships were ablaze off the coast of Oregon.

Meanwhile the crew of the *Suwaharu Maru* were working feverishly to contain *their* fire. Their firefighting crew had pumps and hoses operating within minutes of the collision but their cargo of logs, liberally doused with gasoline, was burning fiercely. They battled the flames all night. At first light, as the Japanese were finally mopping up, a Coast Guard aircraft and two cutters, one carrying a doctor, emerged out of the fog to continue the search for the eleven missing members of the *Mandoil*'s crew.

Having had twelve hours to digest the bad news, the ships' owners and agents were by now busy on the long distance telephones, trying to determine what could be salvaged from this expensive disaster. The *Arthur Foss* was dispatched from Seattle to take the log carrier in tow and, in Victoria, Island Tug & Barge's *Sudbury II* was engaged to go to the aid of the *Mandoil II*. Getting the *Suwaharu Maru* safely into port seemed assured; rescuing the *Mandoil II* appeared much less certain. For this reason the *Sudbury II* was engaged on Lloyd's Open Form.

On the second floor of a low, flat-roofed building on Victoria's waterfront, Robbie Robinson, the company's dispatcher, picked up the phone and began making calls. The first was to the *Sudbury II* herself. Out on a job, she was relieved by another of the company's tugs and sped home. Next Robbie called that indispensable member of the crew, the cook. This man needed all the lead time he could get: he got out a pencil and began filling out order forms. Robbie called suppliers, shore people, the diver and the salvage master and then he got out the crew list and started to look for mates with deep-sea tickets and replacements for people who were taking time off. Within hours the *Sudbury II* had her crew, a full load of fuel and an afterdeck piled with cartons of provisions. She let go her lines and churned out of Victoria Harbour, heading for the Strait of Juan de Fuca.

At 2:00 a.m. on March 2, a blip on the *Sudbury II*'s radar screen promised to be the drifting tanker. Closing in on it, Adrian Bull, the tug's captain, turned on his big carbon arc searchlight and probed the darkness. The *Sudbury II*'s "big light" was secured to the roof of the wheelhouse. It was 39 inches in diameter and, since it operated on the same principles as an arc welder, had that same blinding intensity. Now its white glare illuminated three vessels, the fire-ravaged *Mandoil II*, a US Coast Guard cutter and the tanker *Transoneida*. The master of this last vessel, having got a rich whiff of salvage money, had put three crew members and miles of 3/8-inch heaving line on the *Mandoil II*, hoping to satisfy his legal right to claim salvage. The fact that heaving line is barely heavy enough to tow a dinghy and that they had no other towing gear did not lessen their determination to identify themselves as salvors.

Salvage laws state that no salvor can attempt to salvage a ship without her master's consent. Once consent is obtained, the ship's agent and the salvage company arrange payment either on an hourly basis or on LOF. An abandoned ship like the *Mandoil II*, however, presents another set of circumstances. She is a "derelict" ship, and in this case the first on the scene to get a line aboard may claim to be the salvor and may claim appropriate recompense. The catch here is that the impromptu salvor must show that he can provide remedy. In other words, he can't claim to be a salvor unless he is *capable* of being one.

In the company's Vancouver office, Art Elworthy and Jacques Heyrman were standing by the radio-telephone. Adrian Bull relayed the news that there was already a ship on the scene and that she had a line aboard. He also mentioned that it was a heaving line. Then he edged the *Sudbury II* up close to the *Mandoil II*'s bow to sneak a look at what towing preparations, if any, were taking place on the crippled vessel. Obviously there were none. For the rest of the day the *Sudbury II* drifted around, waiting for the insurers, the agents and Island Tug to sort out the situation. Finally the radio-phone came to life. "Tell them to bugger off," said the Vancouver office.

The starboard side of the steam tanker Mandoil II, *after she collided with another vessel in 1968. Note the melted remains of an aluminum lifeboat, just below the funnel.* Captain Don Horn photo

Advice of a similar nature had reached the crew of the *Transoneida*. They left (to pursue their tenuous claim to salvage via the courts), and the *Sudbury II* began salvage operations. Her deck crew dropped the work boat into the water and Roy Blake, the salvage master, and four others climbed into it and putt-putted across the water to the *Mandoil II*. Climbing over the bulwarks, they found themselves on a deck still hot from the fire that had swept it hours before. Around them the aluminum lifeboats and the bronze valves had melted into puddles; amidships the centre castle was untouched but further aft all was devastation. The aft accommodation was gutted. The windows, the fixtures and the occupants had been consumed in minutes and only gaping spaces remained. Peering into these former cabins, the salvors found nothing left but a few twisted bedsprings and the dreadful burnt smell of death. They had approached the *Mandoil II* in a reasonably cheerful frame of mind but this annihilation cast a pall over them. It was a sombre group that set about making a survey of the tanker.

The Mandoil II *was listing slightly and was riding so low in the water that the sea lapped at her decks.* Captain Don Horn photo

The ship was listing slightly and was riding so low in the water that the sea lapped at her decks. Part of the log carrier's anchor lay beside the gaping tear in her bulwarks. Where that ship had sliced into the *Mandoil II*, the sheerstrake, 1-inch steel plate, was rolled up like a clock spring. In the starboard cargo tanks, 30 feet of water sloshed around in the darkness. The log carrier had struck the *Mandoil II* just behind the fo'c'sle head and had penetrated a third of the ship's width. The remaining deck plates were buckled and cracked by the force of the impact and the ensuing fire. Roy Blake relayed this information to Adrian Bull.

The *Sudbury II*'s captain had been born in Malta. Like several of the Island Tug skippers, he had apprenticed with the British Merchant Service and had received his Foreign Going Master's ticket in Glasgow in 1958. Three years later he was in Victoria working for Island Tug as a seaman. This drop in status was no reflection of his abilities; starting at the bottom was common practice at Island Tug and it gave Adrian a chance to get the tow-boat experience he needed. One of Island Tug's captains explained, "The company had a system of training people. They worked them through the fleet, starting with the 'littlest toot.' That way you were responsible for fewer dollars." Since 1966 Adrian had been responsible for the *Sudbury II*, the largest ship in the fleet, and now he was responsible for the *Mandoil II* as well. Given the damage the forward section of the tanker had sustained, he thought that towing her in the conventional manner might pull her bow off. He decided to tow her stern first.

Just below the *Sudbury II*'s main deck, immediately aft of the towing winch, was the "wire room." Here drum after drum of 1 3/4-inch wire cable was stowed against the bulkheads and enormous shackles, thimbles, clamps and stoppers were lashed neatly in rows. A hatch opened from the wire room onto the afterdeck. Now electric motors fed wire bridles onto the deck and the deck crew began the complicated business of coupling up to a ship with no power. Since the *Mandoil II* wouldn't be able to haul in the massive towing wire with her own winch, the *Sudbury II*'s winch would have to supply the necessary power. A deckhand bent a heaving line onto a heavier manila line and then the heavier line onto the wire bridle. The tug swung around, hung a scant 15 feet off the the tanker's stern and a deckhand flung the heaving line up to the salvage crew. Next came the heavier line, which they passed around the *Mandoil II*'s bitts and then back to the tug. Using the *Sudbury II*'s capstan, the men hauled the rest of the manila line and finally the wire aboard the tanker and secured it to her bitts. The second bridle was similarly connected and then the towline shackled on. The towline paid out and the *Sudbury II* gradually increased her speed and began to pull, with no appreciable effect.

Perhaps in a desperate effort to avoid the collision, the *Mandoil II*'s rudder was jammed hard over. Her steering gear was smashed, and the huge gash in her side trapped the water. She was, as well, ever so slowly sinking. So the *Sudbury II* pulled for hours, heeled over with the effort of trying to get her in line astern while the *Mandoil II*, heedless of all this exertion, wandered off in a direction that she seemed to find more appealing. It was, said George Winterburn, one of the *Sudbury II*'s engineers, more a controlled drift than a tow. And then, just twenty-four hours after they had put their wire on the *Mandoil II*, it parted. Sitting at breakfast, Adrian Bull felt a sudden jerk and didn't need the second mate to tell him what had happened.

"Okay, wind it on in," he said, "and I'll go back and take a look." He finished his coffee and went on deck where the towing winch was already humming in the wire.

At least it's daylight, he told himself, at least it's not raining or blowing. Two years before he had rescued the *Tainan*. The *Tainan* had run out of fuel; they'd even used up their generator fuel so they had no power on deck. The crew had had to pull in the towline by hand and it took them almost four hours, by which time a gale had blown up. For all those hours Adrian had stood back aft at the controls trying to keep the *Sudbury II* 10 to 15 feet off the *Tainan*'s bow. Above him "the little Chinese guys" on deck were hauling away—first manila, then chain, then the towing wire. It was dark, it was raining and it was blowing. Occasionally someone would appear out of the rain and shove a cup of coffee into Adrian's hand. They didn't break his concentration by speaking to him.

The Sudbury II*'s massive chain bridle.* Sheret photo, Seaspan

On the *Mandoil II* the two bridles had chafed themselves apart in the fairlead. The deck crew now hauled chain on deck, fashioned new bridles with it and the heavy laborious job of coupling up began all over again. Used as a bridle, chain has an advantage over wire in that its weight creates a droop or "belly," and this slack acts as a spring.

Once more reconnected, the tug resumed her effort to drag the reluctant *Mandoil II* along behind her. It was like trying to tow Vancouver Island. They were 200 miles off Cape Flattery by this time and the wind had gotten up; it was shrieking through the rigging at a good 60 knots, waves were breaking over the *Mandoil II*'s forward deck and the *Sudbury II* was making no headway at all. She was, in fact, losing ground. Another Island Tug vessel, the *Island Monarch*, set out to assist her.

It was a wild ride for the *Monarch*. Driving along at the best speed she could muster, she was soon out past the relative shelter of the Strait of Juan de Fuca. She was encountering mountainous seas and was taking a terrible beating. "It was a hell of a ride out," said her mate, Jim Derby. "We were just leaping from wave to wave all night. The skipper was Drydie Jones. He said, 'What are you trying to do, kill me?' We had an ex-naval commander or something working as a deckhand. He got so sick he lost his teeth down the toilet. For the rest of the trip he had no teeth."

This weather did nothing to calm the nerves of those on the *Mandoil II*. They had spent their first night in the officers' quarters amidships which, through some freakish accident, had been left untouched by the fire. All night those on watch, flashlights in hand, checked the water in the cargo tanks. Every hour the *Sudbury II* talked to them by radio.

"They were not happy," said George Matson, the *Sudbury II*'s mate. "There was no heat. They were cold, wet, tired and hungry. They sounded bloody miserable."

They were even more miserable when daylight arrived. They had brought an inflatable with them, their means of escape in an emergency, and had hauled it up on the *Mandoil II*'s deck. That deck, however, was still hot from the fire that had swept it so recently and during the night their rubber boat had caught fire and melted away. This did nothing to boost morale. The *Mandoil II*'s load of oil had already demonstrated that given very little encouragement, it could explode like dynamite. Now the crew were effectively marooned on a drifting bomb. Glumly they checked the towing gear for chafing, measured the water in the cargo tanks, noted the deteriorating weather and got increasingly nervous as day became night. The tanker was so low in the water that the seas were sweeping right over her decks. In the dark a slab of plating was wrenched free by the waves, groaned across the deck and dropped into the sea. Sitting there on that cold, dark half-sinking ship, the men discussed the possible outcome awaiting them and tried to decide which would be worse: to sink or to blow up.

Ed Creed had been snatched from his job as shore engineer to fill the *Sudbury II*'s complement. He had never taken part in anything quite like this before and he was fighting panic. The only thing that kept this panic in check was the presence of Roy Blake and Jack Daly, who were old hands. Jack Daly, in particular, was as tough as they come. As long as *they* think it's okay, Ed told himself, then I guess it's okay. And then, somewhere aft, the fire broke out once again.

"Mother of God, save us all," said Jack Daly.

Ed's anxiety reached an all-time high.

Roy Blake picked up his walkie-talkie and called the *Sudbury II*. "This bloody ship's on fire again," he told Adrian. "Get us the hell off."

"The fire on the *Mandoil II* has broken out again," Captain Bull radioed to the Coast Guard vessel that had remained on the scene, "and my guys want off. I don't want to let the towline go, and I sure as hell don't want to go alongside. Could you take your rubber ducky and go in?"

"Anything you want," said the master of the cutter.

The US Coast Guard were well trained, well equipped and endlessly co-operative. Adrian Bull admired "this wonderful bunch of guys" then, and he still does.

The cutter positioned herself upwind of the *Mandoil II*. Her men inflated their life raft and then decided that its canopy, designed to shelter the occupants, was going to impede access to the raft itself. Without a moment's hesitation, they sliced it off. They secured a line to it and launched it. Now the challenge was to drift it to its destination. Trailing it astern of the cutter, they paid out line—enough to get it to the *Mandoil II* but not so much that they lost control of it. The raft rose and fell, planing down the huge waves like a car in a fun fair. Through his binoculars the cutter's captain watched the proceedings. Twenty-foot seas were breaking over the *Mandoil II* and the little knot of salvors waited at the bulwarks of the ship. Suddenly a huge wave surged over the tanker and the men disappeared from sight. Quietly the captain spoke to Adrian Bull on the *Sudbury II*. "I think she's just taken five more guys," he said.

Scrambling to his feet, soaked to the skin, Roy Blake fumbled for his walkie-talkie. "It's okay, Cap," he said. "We're all here."

"I tell you, we were into that inflatable like birds," said Ed Creed.

The seas were so big that any further junketing about in a small boat seemed impractical. The *Sudbury II*'s salvors returned to the cutter and remained there. They had had virtually nothing to eat since the storm began and they fell upon their host's food supply like the starving men they were. Fortunately there were others on the Coast Guard ship who were *not* eating. Ed Creed remembers a long row of toilets in the cutter's washroom; before each one knelt a retching sailor.

Now the Island Tug men waited for one of several eventualities: the *Mandoil II* would explode or she would sink or she would do neither. She did neither. Instead the wind dropped and the storm-battered *Monarch* arrived.

"Okay, guys," radioed Adrian Bull, "get on there and couple up the *Monarch*."

Much closer to the situation than their captain, the salvors approached the tanker with caution. The fire, however, appeared to have burned itself out.

Now there was the *Monarch* to "push things around." She got the *Mandoil II* heading in the right direction and then added her power to that of the *Sudbury II*. Even then it took both tugs and the current that runs northward off Vancouver Island to get the whole entourage moving, for the *Mandoil II* was oozing oil and taking on water and, as a consequence, was now even lower in the water and had developed a 7-degree list to starboard.

Now another problem presented itself. An inspector from the Ministry of Transport had viewed the tow from the air, seen the oil that was escaping from the tanker and notified his superiors. Radio stations reported, very shortly thereafter, that Canadian authorities would not allow the oil-leaking *Mandoil II* within 100 miles of the coastline. Not to be outdone, the American authorities expressed a similar view. To give this message further emphasis, environmental activists took to phoning Captain Bull's wife, Maureen. Her husband, they implied, was one of the villains of this drama and she must not let him bring his tow into Canadian waters. Since Maureen had no influence on her husband when it came to towing, and even less influence with Island Tug, she could do very little to assuage their concerns.

Nonetheless, to someone in authority it must have seemed unreasonable for the *Sudbury II* and the *Monarch* to sail on forever like the *Flying Dutchman*, dragging the *Mandoil II* behind them. So Adrian was given orders not to bring the *Mandoil II* through the Strait of Juan de Fuca, but instead to tow her up the west coast of Vancouver Island and anchor her in the sheltered waters of Muchalat Inlet. Here they put an oil boom around her and then every vessel on the BC coast that would carry oil was commandeered to unload her.

The Sudbury II *towing the "ghost ship," the* Mandoil II. Captain Don Horn photo

When the *Mandoil II*, emptied of oil and degassified, was finally towed into Victoria in late March, the fire's devastation was there for all to see. The once beautiful ship was a scorched ruin. In her davits hung the skeletal frames of her lifeboats; in her hull the water-filled gash was big enough to float a dinghy; her deck was ridged with 3-foot hills and valleys. Her picture was on the front page of the newspapers and she was dubbed, with not unwarranted hyperbole, "the ghost ship."

Long before the *Mandoil II* arrived in Victoria, however, the *Sudbury II* and her crew returned to their home port. British Columbia's capital city is situated on the southern tip of Vancouver Island. Some 460 kilometres long, Vancouver Island tips slightly on a northwest-southeast axis that follows the contours of the mainland coast. This slight angle tucks Victoria well into the Strait of Juan de Fuca and protects it from the open Pacific. It is nonetheless a windy city, beset by winter gales and surrounded by ferocious tides. Its working fleet is grateful for the shelter of its harbour.

The *Sudbury II* rounded Race Rocks and approached the harbour from the west. The breakwater, Ogden Point's deep-sea docks and the Bapco paint factory slipped by off her starboard bow. The harbour narrowed and widened again, forming a triangular basin—Victoria's Inner Harbour. Its beauty is a tribute to the city's founding fathers, who built the picturesque Empress Hotel on a former swamp on the east side of the harbour, the even more picturesque provincial Parliament Buildings on the south side and the pseudo-classical Canadian Pacific Railway building at its entrance. The north side of this harbour leads into the Upper Harbour, a narrow tidal estuary whose entrance is spanned by the Johnson Street Bridge. Just beyond the bridge lay the docks and offices of Island Tug & Barge, the *Sudbury II*'s moorage. This is where it had all begun many years before.

Now, on a day in mid-March 1968, the *Sudbury II* returned to this moorage with an unlikely passenger: a canary in a cage. When the salvage crew had first boarded the *Mandoil II* they found the little bird in the officers' quarters amidships. Jack Daly salvaged it and they named it Phoenix. Through all their vicissitudes—their transfer to the Coast Guard cutter and then to their own ship—Daly carried the cage and its heroic little occupant. Once on board the *Sudbury II*, it proved a mixed blessing.

"It was a singer," explained George Matson. "Once it got over the shock, that bloody bird sang and it sang and it sang. It drove us nuts. In the confines of a small ship you couldn't escape it."

When they disembarked, Daly remained in charge of the canary, but he stumbled. The cage flew open and the bird disappeared into the sky. Quite obviously it was a canary destined for more than a bird's usual share of trauma.

CHAPTER XII

The *Meteor*

"Captain, all you're going to do is roll this ship over. We've got to get the water out of her."

The very nature of marine salvage keeps the rescuer and the rescued at arm's length. At best there will be a groundswell running when they catch sight of each other; more likely the two will meet in the teeth of a gale. And being dashed against the towering steel hull of a good-sized ship has much the same effect as being thrown against a rock bluff, so the rescuer keeps a wary distance and connects with the quarry by shooting a line from one careening deck to the other.

The salvage of the *Meteor*, however, presented a completely opposite set of circumstances. In flat, calm waters the *Sudbury II* was required to come right alongside. This up-close and intimate experience left her crew, stoics that they were, shaken to the core.

The *Meteor* was a small, older Norwegian cruise ship. Each spring and summer she came to Vancouver and cruised to Alaska. In late May 1971 she was returning from one of these trips, guided down the Inside Passage by one of the two BC pilots on board. In the early hours of that perfect spring morning, slipping serenely through the glassy waters of the Strait of Georgia like a great white wedding cake, she seemed to epitomize all that is right with the world. *Her* world, however, was to slip into chaos in the minutes after 3:00 a.m.

The first indication of trouble was a thick column of smoke rolling out of one of the forward scuttles. A fire alarm sounded on the bridge, and within minutes the flames had severed an electrical connection and the *Meteor* had lost radio communication, steerage and some lighting. Instantly Captain Alf Mørner, the *Meteor*'s master, was out of his bunk and on the bridge. Long years of experience had given him the seaman's ability to snap from sleep to fully efficient consciousness. Suddenly, at 3:00 on this beautiful morning, his ship was on fire. His concerns were many: she was carrying sixty-seven passengers, most of them still asleep; she contained numerous fuel tanks, two of which were situated just aft of the fire; the vessel itself was worth many millions of dollars. Following the standard procedure for fire aboard ship, he pressed a button on the bridge and four decks below him watertight doors slid into place and sealed off the burning forward section from the rest of the ship. He stopped the ship and turned her away from the wind. Then, leaving the pilots in charge in the wheelhouse, he plunged down the companionway toward the fire itself.

With radio communication cut off, no other mariners could know of the *Meteor*'s plight. In the chaotic minutes that followed the fire alarm, the radio operator realized that the pilots carried a portable VHF radio, which he used to send out a Mayday alert.

The Strait of Georgia is a busy waterway, and help arrived almost immediately in the form of the Alaskan ferry MV *Malaspina*. The light sleepers among her passengers were wakened by the cessation of her pulsing engines and by shouts and running feet. Those who were curious enough to venture out on deck saw crewmen lowering their ship's lifeboats while other lifeboats, filled with passengers from the *Meteor*, came across the water toward them.

By now there were flames shooting out of the forward portholes of the *Meteor* and her passengers, seeing their "beautiful ship" burning before their eyes, were distressed. They would have been a good deal more distressed had they known what tragedy was unfolding on the ship. But cocooned as they were by their status as passengers, barely inconvenienced, they were comfortably distanced from the events transpiring on board. Most of the *Meteor*'s surviving crew members now joined them and *Malaspina*, unable to render any further assistance, departed for Vancouver.

Two helicopters from Canadian Forces Base Comox hovered overhead; next to arrive were two Canadian Coast Guard cutters, the *Racer* and the *Ready*. And in Vancouver, Seaspan's dispatcher had picked up the Mayday and had set a full-scale rescue operation in motion. Two of the company's tugs, the *La Garde* and the *Le Beau*, were in the vicinity and were advised of the emergency. Half an hour later they had been relieved of their tows and were racing to the scene. At 7:40 a.m. Seaspan's salvage master, Fred Collins, was departing Vancouver harbour on a chartered float plane.

Meanwhile, on the *Meteor*, Captain Mørner was directing the firefighting crew. Ship owners and their agents are loath to commit themselves to a salvage contract unless absolutely necessary and they transmit this reluctance to their captains. As a result captains exhaust every avenue before admitting defeat—witness the captain of the *Makedonia* and his hatch tarpaulin sail. Captain Mørner had moved all of his passengers safely away and the *Racer* and the *Ready* were now alongside, prepared to add their water power to that of the *Meteor*. Captain Mørner expected to be able to deal with the crisis himself. The combined efforts of all three ships' hoses were having little effect on the fire, however. The only visible result was that the water being poured into the ship's hull was causing her to list markedly to starboard.

By 8:10 a.m. Fred Collins' plane was circling the stricken ship; minutes later he was climbing the companionway to her bridge, where he found the two pilots and the *Meteor*'s third mate, but not her master. The salvage master's immediate concern was the cruise ship's ever-increasing starboard list. He knew that many burning vessels, the *Normandie* among them, had been lost not because of fire but because the water pumped into them caused them to capsize. Obviously the *Meteor*'s bilge pumps weren't keeping up with the volume of water gushing from the fire hoses. Collins retraced his steps and went in search of Captain Mørner.

The *Meteor*'s master was by this time a man obsessed, a man barely conscious of what he was doing. He had only one thought in mind: to extinguish the fire, gain access to the fo'c'sle and save the lives of the crew members trapped behind the bulkhead doors. He knew them all—summer after summer the same people had joined the crew for the Alaska run. Frantically his firefighters poured water into every available opening.

Fred Collins threaded his way through coils of hose and introduced himself. "We have two tugs on the way to assist," he said.

Captain Mørner ignored him. His attention remained focussed on the fire.

"Captain, it's almost nine in the morning. That fire has been raging since three. There is no hope for anyone down there."

Captain Mørner finally turned his attention from the hoses to Fred Collins. He had the shipmaster's instinctive distrust of salvage men. Now one of them had appeared from the sky like a metaphorical vulture and was, he felt, forcing himself upon him. "I don't need tugs," he said shortly, "and I've got all the men I need to fight this fire."

"Captain, there is no way you're going to get into that fo'c'sle," said Collins. "All you're going to do is roll this ship over. We've got to get the water out of her."

For the first time since the fire broke out Captain Mørner became aware of the passage of time. He could feel the slant of the deck under his feet. He knew Fred Collins was right.

"We'll have to do this on LOF," said Seaspan's salvage master.

"We will discuss that later," said the *Meteor*'s master.

By 9:20 a.m. the tug *La Garde* had arrived and her portable pumps were pressed into service as auxiliary bilge pumps, but neither these nor the *Meteor*'s pumps were able to remove any appreciable amount of water from the bilges. The problem, it appeared, was that the scuppers and drains were plugged with debris. Part of this "debris" consisted of dead bodies, a horror that had not yet become apparent to the rescuers. Captain Mørner had made no mention of loss of life, but Fred Collins had noted bodies laid out on the "A" deck rotunda and had drawn his own conclusions.

Throughout the afternoon men poured water into the ship and other men attempted to pump it out. They were breaking portholes now to get at the flames and cutting holes in the bulkheads to allow the water to disperse. And still the fire raged in the alleyways that honeycombed the fo'c'sle. The ship was listing 15 degrees to starboard. "Even Captain Mørner realized that he wasn't getting any results with those damned water hoses," said Seaspan's salvage master. They needed a more sophisticated fire suppressant, and it was on its way.

The cruise ship Meteor *on fire, May 1971. Men poured water in; others attempted to pump it out.* Commercial Illustrators Ltd. photo, Seaspan

At 8:00 that morning, at the same time that Fred Collins was sizing up the situation from his chartered plane, in Victoria the *Sudbury II* was loading gear, fuel, provisions and her Hi-Expansion foam machine, and her crew was climbing aboard. By 9:25 a.m. Donald Elworthy had reached Norwegian Veritas in New York and had finalized a salvage agreement with the shipping agent. At 10:30 a.m. the *Sudbury II* swept out of the harbour.

The *Sudbury II*'s top speed was 13 knots, but now in the engine room her engineers tried to coax a little more than that out of the Cooper-Bessemers. The rising crescendo of those thirty-two cylinders cranking up to the max produced a staccato rap—"a very macho sound," as one of her engineers described it, "a real adrenalin rush." Still, pounding away at a record-breaking speed, it was seven hours before she was within sight of the *Meteor*. Ahead the big white ship lay slumped on her starboard side, attended by the two trim tugs and the flag-scarlet *Ready*. It would have been a picture-postcard scene except for the list and the smoke that billowed out of the *Meteor*'s forward section and blackened her immaculate white paint. On her low side the lifeboats had been launched to reduce top weight and the lines from their davits trailed down into the water. At her bow the *Ready*, advised not to put any more water into her, was playing her powerful hoses on the hull itself, trying to cool down the hot spots.

There was the sharp ratchet ring of the *Sudbury II*'s telegraph and her engines slowed. Jake Derksen stood at the bow, the headline coiled in his hand. As the *Sudbury II* slid alongside, Jake aimed his line for a bollard, threw it—and then felt his recent dinner come surging up in his throat.

"Oh Jesus, Jesus," he said.

Just below the bollard, protruding from a porthole, was a man's head and one arm. They were as black as coal.

The men on the *Sudbury II* now set out to accomplish what the crews of the *Meteor*, the *La Garde*, the *Le Beau*, the *Racer* and the *Ready* had been attempting to do for the last fourteen hours: put out a fire that was burning with increased ferocity and, at the same time, pump out the ship herself. They attempted to wrestle

A picture-postcard scene gone terribly wrong. Left to right: Tugs Le Beau *and* La Garde, *the* Meteor, *the Coast Guard cutter* Ready. Commercial Illustrators Ltd. photo, Seaspan

their big pumps, pipes and hoses onto the *Meteor* and were met with decks that were stove-lid hot. Undeterred, they hauled sheets of plywood from the *Sudbury II*'s woodworking room, threw them down on the deck and marched forward. Scattered around them on the deck, twisted into grotesque shapes by the heat, lay women's shoes.

The *Sudbury II* was using her foam machine for the first time. Her crew stuck its three-foot canvas hose down a companionway and Bob Gray, one of the *Sudbury II*'s engineers, set up a 5-gallon can of foam compound and watched as it mixed with water and was blown into the hose. Then he turned his attention to the pumps. Manhandled into position, these immensely powerful pumps were discharging nothing more than a trickle of water. Bob investigated. He found that the water on the starboard side was within inches of the portholes and that all manner of debris—clothes, bedding and, to his dismay, bodies—was floating around, clogging the intakes for the pumps. Bob Gray was a first-rate engineer: during his career he had coped with typhoons and every conceivable mechanical problem, and he was calm and capable. But his calm, at least, was threatening to desert him. Never in his wildest imaginings could he have envisioned himself wrestling a body away from a pump intake. "Our guys were trying to function," he said. "All we could do was move these bodies out of the way. They were buoyant. They were floating all around. There was one big fella, must have weighed almost 300 pounds. I had an awful time with him."

Hour after hour, while the crew struggled to keep the pumps going, the foam machine continued to blast foam into the forward part of the ship. At first they directed it into hatches and portholes and down companionways. "We ran foam and ran foam and ran foam," said Fred Collins. "It would seek out any opening so we plugged them with anything we could get a hold of. Finally we got her cooled down enough that Jack Daly and I could put on air-breathing equipment and go below."

The fire, they discovered, had come within a hair's breadth of jumping the bulkhead separating the crew's quarters from the main body of the ship. Immediately abaft this bulkhead were the fuel tanks that had leapt into Captain Mørner's mind early that morning. Wood-panelled alleyways extended aft from this bulkhead. The heat was so intense that the varnish on the panelling was smoking and running down the walls; the shower heads in the washrooms were red-hot, as were the steel watertight doors. Fred Collins couldn't help but imagine the lot of the men behind those doors. "You knew that everybody down here would have fled up on deck the minute the fire was discovered. Nobody would have been around to hear those people pound on those steel doors."

Almost seventeen hours after it began, the fire was under control, and the area had cooled down enough to allow the firefighters to turn their attention to the fo'c'sle itself in an effort to find the source of the fire. The *Sudbury II*'s crew, unaware of the sequence of events that had preceded their arrival, weren't prepared for what lay ahead. The watertight doors were opened for the first time since the captain had closed them. Bodies, stacked like cord wood, lay against the unrelenting metal that had barred

The bulkhead separating the crew's quarters from the main body of the ship. RCMP photo, Seaspan

their exit. The *Sudbury II*'s men could barely get inside for bodies. Slipping and sliding over charred limbs, they dragged their canvas hose into the far reaches of the fo'c'sle.

"It was so damned dark," said Jake Derksen. "When everything is charred black, light doesn't illuminate. And then I'd step on something and look down and it was somebody's leg—all black with a bone sticking out. Man, oh, man, I tell you . . . The stuff came off on your hands . . . and the smell, the godawful smell. Somebody told us to remove the bodies but that was it for me. I said, 'Like hell. We don't take the bodies out.'"

By now the *Sudbury II*'s supply of Hi-Ex foam compound was almost exhausted. The Canadian Armed Forces Base at Comox

Fire damage in the passageway in forward "A" deck. RCMP photo, Seaspan

offered a supply of a different type. It was rushed to the scene by speedboat but it turned out to be unsuitable. The Vancouver Fire Department offered the correct chemical and the *Island Champion* picked up their entire supply, 140 gallons of it, and raced to the *Meteor*. She arrived at 4:00 a.m. The new infusion of foam finally brought the fire under control.

Dawn was breaking, and curious onlookers were beginning to circle the ships in a variety of craft. Bob Gray found a tarpaulin and hung it over the side of the *Meteor*. The grisly sight that had first met Jake Derksen's eyes was no longer in public view.

For the first time in more than twenty-four hours there was a pause in the frenzied activity on the *Meteor* and those involved could stop, have a cigarette and reflect on the tragedy that surrounded them. Bob Gray found himself talking to the *Meteor*'s carpenter, a crew member who had stayed aboard to fight the fire.

"A thing like this sure makes a person a fatalist," said the carpenter.

"You think so?"

"Yes," said the carpenter. His words were slow and careful. "I have a girlfriend on this ship. Last night I wasn't in my cabin forward, I was with her, in her cabin, at the stern of the ship. So I'm still alive."

It appears that the wages of sin are not always death, Bob reflected.

Jake Derksen had found a spot in the *Meteor*'s barber shop where he, too, could sit down for a few minutes and have a much-needed cigarette. "I tell you, my nerves were just shot," he said. As he sat gathering his wits he realized that stretched out in a nearby barber chair, inadequately covered by the barber's white cloth, was the body of a man. Oh hell, thought Jake, getting up, I can't take any more of this stuff. Before he was out the door, however, the body rose up and pulled the sheet off its face. Jake had disturbed the exhausted Captain Mørner, who was also seeking some small refuge from the horror.

The fire wasn't extinguished but it was under control. Captain Mørner, the salvage master and the foreman of the salvage team surveyed the situation. They decided the time had come to get underway for Vancouver, so a little flotilla proceeded toward that harbour: the *Island Champion* towing the cruise ship's six lifeboats, the *Meteor*—still listing, but under her own power—and the *Sudbury II* escorting.

At 12:00 noon on May 23 the *Meteor* was made fast at Burrard Dry Dock in Vancouver. Waiting for them there were the Vancouver Fire Department, the RCMP and officials from the coroner's office. The *Sudbury II* moored alongside, her portable pumps once more extracting water from the still-listing cruise ship. All night her pumps roared away. And then, in the morning, the last act of the tragedy took place. The fire department arrived with a large container. With one of the *Meteor*'s deck officers standing by, the firemen hauled out blackened bodies and placed them in the container while the mate, tears coursing down his face, identified those he could. In all, thirty-four crew members had been killed by the fire. Captain Mørner did not come on deck.

Jake Derksen had never stopped to think that someone must deal with the unimaginable horrors that are the aftermath of such emergencies, but he thought about it now. "My God, those firemen, they are some tough," he said.

The *Sudbury II*, finally released from her duties, let go her lines and headed for Victoria. She arrived at 10:00 a.m. on May 24. She and her crew had been away for forty-eight hours. Heather Gray drove down to pick up her husband.

"Robert is a very calm man," she said, "but he couldn't stop talking. He was so wired. I've never seen him like that in his life; he just talked for hours and hours." In today's society the *Sudbury II*'s crew would have been offered the services of counsellors or trauma teams after an event such as the *Meteor* salvage. In 1971 Bob Gray had to come to terms with this tragedy on his own.

"It was what you call a 'marine incident'," he said finally. "And I guess that's what we're there for—marine incidents."

CHAPTER XIII

The *Vanlene*

"You have to work fast to save what you can before the sea snatches it away from you."

Over almost twenty years the two *Sudburys* had brought every ship in their care into port safely. It was an astonishing record, given the conditions that usually prevailed and given the fact that neither the captains nor the crews had ever done deep-sea towing or salvage before. They had hauled their charges through typhoons and hurricanes, had reconnected their towlines working up to their waists in waves and had fought their fires. They had overcome a Greek captain's stubborn resistance to being salvaged and had yanked him and his ship off a reef with brute force. They had employed batteries of pumps, helicopters and a Hi-Ex Foam machine. But it was not until they salvaged the *Mandoil II* that they were introduced to oil booms and the degassifying of fuel tanks. Not until the *Mandoil* did environmental concerns play a part in the *Sudburys*' rescues.

The *Mandoil II* had been barred from entering Victoria harbour and was redirected to Muchalat Inlet, where she was secured and her cargo pumped out into a hastily assembled collection of oil barges. In the four years following her salvage, environmental protection had become ever more important. In 1972 there was not yet a Ministry of the Environment as such; environmental protection fell under the Ministry of Transport's jurisdiction and that body carried out its new role with zeal, as the *Sudbury II* was to discover.

In the middle of March that year the *Sudbury II* was still on the Rock Run. Adrian Bull, her captain, announced his arrival in Blubber Bay to the dispatcher in Victoria and was preparing to position his empty barge for loading when his routine was rudely interrupted.

"We've got a ship on the rocks on the west coast," said the dispatcher, "Motor Vessel *Vanlene*. Drop the barge and get down here ASAP. We need a quick start."

By the time the *Sudbury II* reached Victoria, Seaspan and the owner's representative had agreed that the *Sudbury II* would be dispatched to the aid of Captain Loh Chung Hong's vessel, the 8,000-ton MV *Vanlene*, under the terms of LOF. And in Victoria, one thing became abundantly clear: pollution control would figure largely in this salvage.

Within hours of the ship's grounding, the Ministry of Transport had contacted Seaspan and laid down the law—Section 741 of the Canadian Shipping Act, to be exact. They told the company that the *Vanlene* was not to be removed unless anti-pollution equipment was on the scene. Should the salvors disregard this advice, and as a result cause an oil spill, they would be considered negligent and they would be prosecuted.

Seaspan had no intention of disregarding this advice. In the Salvage Depot in Victoria they assembled two 600 CFM compressors and pumps, five 164-foot sections of TT oil boom, ten 45-gallon containers of Gamelen Sea Clean and various other pumps, hoses and spray nozzles.

Meanwhile Roy Blake, the salvage master, sifted through the conflicting reports received by the Rescue Co-ordination Centre and tried to determine the exact position of the *Vanlene*. The tug *Neva Straits* had the last word on this matter. She and another tug had removed the *Vanlene*'s crew, she reported, and the ship herself was aground adjacent to the southwest side of Austin Island in Barkley Sound.

It was at this point that Roy was informed that he would not be the sole supervisor of the *Vanlene*'s salvage. He was joined by two other men: the Ministry of Transport's rather grandly named On Scene Commander—in another life the Steamship Inspector—and this man's On Scene Advisor. The three headed for Barkley Sound on an MOT helicopter. Right behind them came the *Sudbury II*.

The *Vanlene* had grounded on the evening of March 14. By noon of the next day, circling the wreck in the helicopter, the three men found her lodged on a shoal. Her forefoot was at the waterline; her stern was submerged and awash forward to the aft end of the midship house work. The tug *Neva Straits*, the first to come to the *Vanlene*'s assistance, was standing by. A phone call to the ship's Chief Engineer, who had been landed in Ucluelet, determined that the vessel contained approximately 450 tons of fuel at the time of grounding and was carrying a cargo of several hundred new automobiles. An oil slick was moving away toward the Broken Islands. That evening the *Sudbury II* picked up Roy Blake in Bamfield and by just after midnight she was anchored off the *Vanlene*.

Roy Blake had been a captain since his early twenties and had been the salvage master in the *Mandoil* rescue and a dozen other salvage jobs. As a salvor he had been thrown into all kinds of crises, each one unique except for the requirement that he save the ship in question, if possible, or if not, to save as much of her cargo as he could. He was used to thinking on his feet, acting quickly and decisively. Now he found himself in a position noted for both its inefficacy and its cheerlessness—that of a committee member. Two government vessels were on hand by now, the Coast Guard cutter *Ready* and the *Laymore*. The On Scene Commander, the On Scene Advisor, the masters and chief officers of the aforementioned vessels and Roy boarded the *Laymore* for a meeting. Before long they were joined by the master and chief officer of the *Camsell*, a third government vessel. The meeting pressed on. Logistics and lines of authority were clarified; the *Camsell* was designated as the On Scene Commander's vessel,

The 8,000-ton Vanlene, *her stern submerged and awash forward to the aft end of the midship house work, March 1972.* Bill Roozeboom photo, Seaspan

with the other government vessels being deployed as required; the On Scene Commander's Advisor was assigned to oversee all work aboard the *Vanlene*; the *Sudbury II* was assigned the responsibility of oil removal and was advised to have her motor lifeboat and rubber boat in readiness at daylight. It was beginning to sound, Roy reflected, like the assault on Omaha Beach.

By 7:00 on the morning of March 16, the crew of the *Sudbury II* reported that their boat and inflatable were launched and ready. The assembled inspection team was divided into two units. The first was to board the *Vanlene* and conduct a detailed inspection of the vessel; the second was to take soundings around and alongside her since the divers from the *Laymore* reported that they were unable to conduct an underwater survey due to the heavy surge factor.

At 10:00 a.m., when these tasks had been completed, the two teams repaired to the *Sudbury II* and prepared charts of the soundings of the holds and tanks. Calls were now coming in from Bennett Pollution Controls and the MOT regarding further pollution control equipment. At 11:30 a.m. a marine surveyor arrived and he and Roy resounded the tanks.

Thus far the weather had remained fair; only a low swell rolled past the *Vanlene*. But March is not a particularly tranquil month on the west coast, and by noon an increasing swell forced the *Sudbury II* to move to a more sheltered anchorage. Roy wondered just how long their luck would hold. Speed is essential in salvage operations. "You have to work fast to save what you can before the sea snatches it away from you," said Fred Collins, Seaspan's fleet services manager. "Roy knew that."

For the next few hours additional tugs and an Okanagan Helicopter were kept busy transporting a Slick Licker, pumpmen and pollution technicians to the scene. And further surveys, assessments and meetings took place. The weather continued to deteriorate and turbulence caused by the sea and the reef made diving too dangerous. By this time, however, the general consensus was that salvaging the hull was probably impossible.

At 9:00 a.m. on March 17 the *Sudbury II* relayed this message to Captain Dick Tolhurst at Seaspan's head office in Vancouver. Later that day, having conferred with the vessel's owners, Dick Tolhurst contacted Roy to tell him that it had been agreed that Seaspan would abandon any effort to salvage the ship's hull and would, instead, concentrate all efforts on saving the cargo. Roy had by this time formed a plan for salvaging this cargo and for removing the 150 tons of oil that were now all that remained on board. He proposed that a helicopter be hired to airlift the cars from the *Vanlene*'s holds and load them onto a barge. They agreed that Effingham Anchorage, a mile from the point of grounding, would be an ideal place to moor the barge. Once the holds were clear of cargo, Roy proposed to cut a hole in their decks and remove the oil in the tanks underneath by whatever means seemed most practical. The Vancouver office sprang into action. They negotiated terms with Okanagan Helicopters, ordered a barge to proceed to Effingham Anchorage, obtained two sets of car hoists, provided stowage plans and asked for confirmation of hatch sizes.

By 6:30 a.m. on March 18 the salvors were on board the *Vanlene*, making plans for the removal of her cargo. She was a ship equipped with "goal posts": four sets of twin masts that rose up like goalposts, down the length of her hull. With derricks these provided an efficient system for loading and unloading cargo. With a flooded engine room and no hope of getting power to the winches, however, these posts were not only useless but a hazard to any helicopter that hovered above. Roy Blake and his group proposed to lift the cargo booms out of their cradles and wing them outboard. Then they would cut the goal posts between No. 1 and No. 2 holds and drop them onto the fo'c'sle head. They would then repeat the process, cutting the goalposts between No. 2 and No. 3 holds and dropping them against the bridge. The whole procedure resembled nothing so much as a logging operation, and posed its attendant risks. These were not trees, after all, but towering masts 8$^{1}/_{2}$ inches in circumference, made of 1-inch steel.

At 10:45 a.m. Roy and the On Scene Advisor boarded the *Camsell* for their daily meeting with the On Scene Commander. Within minutes their hopes of salvaging the cargo and the fuel that lay under it were dashed. They were instructed that all attempts to salvage the cargo must cease until the oil pollution control was completed. The On Scene Commander drove this point home when he commandeered the ordered helicopter to transport pumps and barrels over to the *Vanlene*. Roy argued his case but it was futile. He failed to realize that the salvage plans had to satisfy the bureaucrats in Ottawa. There were planes flying overhead now, and pictures appearing in the newspapers. Politicians have learned that it is not the event itself but the public's perception of it that guarantees their longevity in office. Roy's plan to save all those little Dodge Colts carried the taint of commercialism, or perhaps expediency. In fact, salvaging the cars and then the oil would have been accomplished most efficiently in that order. But the On Scene Commander made it quite clear that the oil must be removed before the cargo.

To execute this operation the *Sudbury II*'s crew would have to connect with one or other of the pipes that ran down into the oil tanks and then pump the oil up to the deck where it could be directed into a barge. There were filler pipes, bleeder pipes and sounding pipes running from deck level down three decks to the tanks. The *Sudbury II*'s engineers chose the most suitable of these and set about making flanges to connect the pipes to pumps. But before they could complete this procedure, another problem arose.

Oil booms had been arriving in a steady stream and were now deployed around the Broken Islands. The weather was continuing to deteriorate, however, and waves were washing over the booms, carrying oil with them. These same waves made it impossible to bring a barge alongside the *Vanlene*. The On Scene Commander decided that until the weather moderated, the oil would be pumped into empty barrels. At the taxpayers' expense, empty oil drums began to rain from the sky, courtesy of Okanagan Helicopters. At this point someone mentioned that it was quite possible for the weather to remain inclement for days and that if this were the case, it would take approximately ten days to remove the oil this way, providing they could get the pumps to work. It was also noted that some of the empty drums had no tops, making them highly unsatisfactory containers. The On Scene Advisor then requested permission from his superiors to burn the oil or, as an alternative, to pump it into inflatable bags called dracons. These alternative arrangements, they were informed, would require Ottawa's approval, which would be forthcoming in a day or two.

Roy Blake went back to the *Sudbury II*. He called Dick Tolhurst and reported that there was very little oil in the vicinity, as it had been pretty well dispersed by nature and the Slick Licker. He said that the barge at Effingham Anchorage was dragging due to the wind. He relayed the latest weather report, which predicted gales. And, Roy thought wearily as he put the radiophone back in its cradle, if we don't get our asses in gear pretty soon, we're going to lose the bundle.

The gales didn't materialize but next day the seas were still too high to board the *Vanlene* with safety. Seaspan and the MOT scoured the Lower Mainland and the Puget Sound area for a barge small enough to get alongside the *Vanlene* without impaling itself on the rocks surrounding the grounded vessel. And the On Scene Commander called out the helicopter and went off to observe the oil slick wending its way through the islands.

By early afternoon the wind had abated enough for a crew to board the freighter. The *Sudbury II*'s engineers had fabricated the required flanges, and had proceeded to couple up a 2-inch pump and attempted to pump, without success. "We found that when we had prime, all we were able to pump was water," said the salvage report. "Eventually we lost prime completely and even though we pumped water into the lower end of the tank we could not force oil or water up the vent to prime." The amount of oil recovered at the end of the day was discouragingly small and the reason soon became clear: with no heater coils working, the oil had solidified into tar. So the crew put Gamelen, a solvent, down the pipes in an effort to thin the material in the tanks. Now they found themselves putting clean Gamelen down the pipes and pumping dirty Gamelen out of them while the oil stayed intact.

By March 20 the wind had dropped and conditions seemed safe enough for Jack Daly to do an underwater survey, which confirmed that the hull of the *Vanlene* was not salvageable. The pumping team continued their efforts to remove oil from the tanks. The *Seaspan Challenger* arrived with a small barge. The *Sudbury II*'s engineers worked at making up and installing more pipe connections. And the *Seaspan Navigator* departed for Bamfield to pick up provisions, fresh water and the requested second cook to help cater for the assembled crowd.

The pumpmen continued to experiment with pumps and pumping combinations. They tried cutting an opening in the hull and, using the Bennett Vacuum pump, finally appeared to be picking up oil; however, before long they were pumping water as before. They moved the pump to the engine room space, which proved to be more successful, and pumped there for the rest of the day, loading the oil into several small barges that had arrived.

It was now March 21—a week since the actual grounding. Whether it was a Freudian slip caused by one too many meetings or simply a slip can't be determined, but in any event Roy Blake slipped on the Jacob's ladder when boarding the *Vanlene* and hurt his leg. Fred Collins, the company's fleet services manager, came out to relieve him. Before Roy left, however, he boarded the government vessel with Fred Collins and the On Scene Advisor for another meeting with the On Scene Commander. Both Seaspan captains pleaded their case: of the 450 tons of oil on the ship when she grounded, 250 had escaped and they had spent the last five days trying, with varying degrees of success, to remove the remainder. They argued that the pollution control had been completed and that they should now be allowed to turn their attention to their customer's interests. They did not press the point that during the week they had spent on the scene the *Vanlene* had continued to settle and her cargo holds fill with water. Cargo that could have been salvaged within the first twenty-four hours was now damaged beyond repair. Okanagan Helicopters had estimated that they could remove one car every few minutes, so in a very short time most of the cargo could have been removed and the salvors would then have had relatively easy access to the oil tanks.

"That word 'salvage' was the problem," said Fred Collins. "Just stop and think about it. Everything a salvor looks at has potential value. It's in his best interests to save everything he can and that very fact makes a salvor a good pollution control person. But say the word 'salvage' and it got their hackles up right away."

By March 23 even the On Scene Commander had to admit that nothing more was being pumped out of the *Vanlene*'s bowels, and the *Sudbury II* was officially released from her pollution control duties. That didn't prevent the MOT people from planning yet another inspection for the next day, however. Fortunately the weather intervened; it was too rough to board the *Vanlene* and the On Scene Commander and his entourage finally departed. The *Sudbury II* and the *Seaspan Navigator* spent the day loading the barges with pollution control equipment and lashing it down. And then, in the late afternoon, ignoring the still high seas, the salvage crew from the *Sudbury II* climbed aboard the *Vanlene* and took stock of the situation they now faced.

The vessel was by this time listing quite markedly and each time a swell hit her she shuddered visibly. She lay on two under-

The Sudbury II*'s crew cut away the* Vanlene*'s No. 2 port forward derrick, lifted the beams and opened the upper 'tween deck hatch.* Bill Roozeboom photo, Seaspan

water ridges of rock and was settling more rapidly than they would have liked. The cargo in her afterholds was awash with seawater.

By next morning the weather was calm and clear and the swell decreasing. At 6:00 a.m. the salvage crew climbed into the motor lifeboat with their cutting tools, left the *Sudbury II* in Effingham Anchorage and putt-putted across to the grounded ship. Within an hour they had cut away the No. 2 port forward derrick, lifted the beams and opened the upper tween deck hatch and cut away aft No. 2 port and starboard derricks. Then Jake Derksen, the former high-lead logger, turned his attention to the goalposts. "He dropped them just as if they were trees," said Fred Collins. "We put a line up on the crosspiece and then a block and tackle down to the tug, which kept the strain. And then he just cut. They fell the way of the strain—right where we wanted them."

The crew dropped the "goalposts" as if they were trees. Bill Roozeboom photo, Seaspan

By 12:30 p.m. the *Seaspan Ranger* had arrived with a barge and secured it alongside the *Sudbury II* at Effingham Anchorage. An hour later there was a helicopter clattering away overhead. A hundred feet above the *Vanlene* the pilot positioned his craft precisely above hold No. 2 and his crew lowered a sling, which four men in the hold hooked around a white Dodge Colt. Minutes later the little car sailed skyward, traversed a mile of water and landed gently on the barge. It was a powerful aircraft and it was operating at close quarters; each time it came down to pick up a car it nearly blew those on deck into the sea.

The helicopter pilot positions his craft a hundred feet above the Vanlene. *Four men hooked a sling around a Dodge Colt and minutes later the little car sailed skyward.* Bill Roozeboom photo, Seaspan

At 6:30 p.m. darkness put an end to the day's successful airlift. By that time thirty-four brightly coloured cars were lined up on the barge and the *Sudbury II*'s crew had an unreserved admiration for the two helicopter pilots who worked in relays.

Fred Collins was able to report to Vancouver that the loaded barge was on its way and that an empty one was already in place for the next day's work. He advised the office that the helicopter was moving one car every seven minutes and being refuelled after every seventh car. It was taking thirty to forty-five minutes for the helicopter to go to Ucluelet to refuel, a time that was to be reduced by having fuel flown in and put on one of the barges. To take advantage of a maximum hatch opening, they had cut through the bulkhead and had driven the cars from No. 3 upper tween decks into No. 2 tween decks. Some of the vehicles had sustained damage, which he listed—one windshield, one bumper, one door panel.

It was March 26, almost two weeks since the grounding, and the weather continued to hold. By 6:00 a.m. the salvage team were once more aboard the *Vanlene*, ready to repeat the previous day's performance. They removed No. 3 derrick and cut away No. 2 and No. 3 goalposts. The block and tackle to the tug forced the wreckage over the side, leaving No. 3 hatch clear for the helicopter. It was just like logging, Jake Derksen reflected. By 10:40 a.m. the goalposts were down and Jake was in the hold ready to help secure the slings. At the end of the day forty-three cars had been safely transferred to the barge.

By the third day of the operation, those in the hold had worked their way downward. "Three decks down that hatch opening looked pretty small," said Jake. "At the bottom we were running into rocks. And the back end of the ship was screeching and grinding. It wasn't very pleasant. If anything had gone wrong we would never have got out of there."

Fred Collins had been instructed by the insurance company that "if sea water has touched metal we don't want it." The cars that were now emerging bore witness to the fact that the men in the hold were now scraping the bottom of the barrel, literally and figuratively. The airlift was over; they had saved 131 cars. An equal number remained in the afterholds, awash in varying depths of oily water. By noon on March 28 the *Sudbury II* had departed for Victoria; the *Vanlene* was officially abandoned.

Since the days of sail, salvage has proved an irresistible opportunity to improve one's lot. Long before radar or DF, someone invented the marine equivalent of pit-lamping. On stormy nights they tied a lantern around a donkey's neck and led the animal along a rocky shore. To unwitting mariners the bobbing light appeared to be another ship with several fathoms of water under her. Thus misled into thinking the shore to be more distant than it was, they were lured onto the rocks, where the crew were left to the sea and the cargo was salvaged by the locals. Since then, of course, the world has become more complex, and salvage a good deal more civilized. Salvage rules have been codified and are now enforced by international law. An abandoned ship, however, remains an abandoned ship and is available to all. And an abandoned ship known to contain dozens of brand-new cars sparks the entrepreneurial spirit in the most unlikely people. Now fish boats with tackle capable of lifting 2,000 pounds waited for high tide and then came alongside the *Vanlene*. They swung their booms over a hatch, put some lengths of good strong manila under a car and in no time at all a Dodge Colt swung through the air and was guided onto the back deck. Nor were those with lighter rigging excluded from this bonanza. They disassembled the cars and loaded them piecemeal. And there were those that showed a preference for batteries. A small village with no road has little use for cars but it can use any number of good storage batteries. Finally the salvors fell upon the *Vanlene*'s teak decks. It was hard work, for decks are securely fastened down and teak is an extremely heavy wood but they persevered and gradually the decks disappeared along with all the other removable material. Before the ship eventually broke up and sank, a great deal of material had found its way into private hands. Scruples, however, prevented those best equipped to benefit from this largesse from doing so: the two helicopter pilots, having salvaged everything acceptable to the insurance adjusters, resisted, with some difficulty, the temptation to pick up two of the rejected automobiles and whisk them away to a secluded but accessible spot.

CHAPTER XIV

Parbuckling at Amchitka

"They had a hell of a good time. They saw the whole Aleutian chain."

Captain "Buster" Fransvaag is a huge man. He towers over the rest of the populace like a great shaggy Viking—which, of course, he is. It takes no stretch of the imagination to envision him wading ashore on some bleak windswept beach, with a helmet on his head and a bearskin flung over his shoulders, leading a group of Norsemen. But in 1974 he wasn't doing anything quite that dramatic. He was, instead, commanding the *Sudbury II* and his crew were not Vikings but experienced towboat men. He himself was an outstanding seaman, he had two competent mates, an excellent cook and a Chief Engineer whose cheerful English matter-of-factness perfectly balanced Buster's Norse melodrama.

The *Sudbury II*'s skipper had trained in the Norwegian Navy and its rigid hierarchy had left him with a permanent distaste for the idea that officers, and especially captains, were exalted beings. Buster valued all his crew members equally, placing himself among them, and he put his philosophy into practice when he took command of the *Sudbury II*. One of the first things he did was eliminate the officer's mess room. "This isn't the navy," he said. "We sail together—we eat together." And so, in April 1974, they sailed for Japan.

Towing across the Pacific was nothing new for the *Sudbury II*, of course, although this was the first such trip since the 1960s. What made this voyage unusual was that completing it required three captains, relays of crew members, a good deal of medical attention, squads of divers and a couple of insurance adjusters. On that late April evening, however, as their vessel emerged from the Strait of Juan de Fuca into a light northwest wind, her crew were blissfully unaware of these imminent ramifications.

The *Sudbury II* was towing two barges heavily laden with packaged lumber and logs. Captain Fransvaag laid out a course for Unimak Pass and they headed north, followed the chain of Aleutian Islands and then curved down toward Tokyo. They dropped the smaller barge and continued on into the Inland Sea with the larger one, the *Ketchikan*.

The stretch of water from Osaka to Fukuyama is the busiest part of this already overcrowded waterway and there is no traffic control. The *Sudbury II* asked for a Japanese pilot for this portion of the trip but this request was somehow overlooked and no pilot was forthcoming. So the tug, with her enormous barge in tow, set off through the confusion of marine traffic without assistance. It was an unnerving experience. At any one time there were eight or ten deep-sea ships and half a hundred fishing boats around the tug, all travelling at speed through a narrow waterway. Peter Davies, the Chief Engineer, watched transfixed as a container vessel whistled by on one side and a tanker on the other. The *Sudbury II*'s barge was their salvation, however. The *Ketchikan* did not tow straight. She yawed wildly from one side to the other and periodically, when vessels came too close, she took a run at them. No doubt word was passed by radio to keep clear of this temperamental monster.

When the *Sudbury II* had delivered the second of her barges to

The Sudbury II *towing the* Ketchikan, *loaded with logs and bound for Japan, 1974.* Seaspan

its destination there was a wait of several weeks while they were both unloaded and reloaded with pipe bound for the Alaska oil pipeline development at Prudhoe Bay. This pause provided a respite for the crew, many of whom spent their time in the nearest bar. For some of them this was not a particularly good idea. The cook was the first casualty. Returning from a night of revelry he fell off the gangplank into the water.

"Paddy," he bleated, clinging to the fender log. "P-a-a-a-ddy."

One of his inebriated shipmates, who had safely negotiated the gangplank, staggered over to the ship's side, stared down at the inky water and delivered his considered opinion.

"If I were you," he said, "I'd forget Paddy. I'd yell 'Help'."

The cook was rescued but his glasses were not, so that when he returned in the same condition the following night he failed to *see* the gangplank and went straight in off the dock. When he was pulled out the second time, they found he had barked all the skin off his shins. Buster, who prized his good cooking, hustled him to a doctor but it was no use. His wounds would need considerable time to heal, the doctor said, so the cook was flown home to Victoria. Buster mourned his loss, especially since his replacement, a young American who was advertised as a short-order cook, turned out to know nothing at all about cooking, short or otherwise.

"It was a logistical fiasco on my part," said Buster. "I should never have accepted the man. Maybe I was panicking. We were getting near typhoon season and with a tow like that I wanted to get going."

Before they could do that, however, they had another casualty among the crew members. An oiler went ashore one night and returned at 9:30 the next morning looking like the sole survivor of Custer's last stand. He was late for his watch, but he turned to, so the Chief overlooked this transgression. As Ray Sundby recalls, speaking of an earlier voyage, "The rule regarding the firemen's drinking was that as long as they could slide down the ladder into the boiler room they were fit to work." However, by noon this man was obviously in such bad shape that Peter told him to go and lie down. Next morning he presented himself and said, "I think I have to see a doctor."

"What's the matter?"

"Well, it's my teeth." He demonstrated his problem by grabbing his lower teeth and moving them from a vertical to a horizontal position.

"I think you've got a broken jaw," said Peter, surveying this distressing spectacle. "We'd better go up and see Buster."

Closer questioning by his captain revealed that he had not only a broken jaw but "holes in his head," as he put it, and double vision. Someone had obviously struck him with the proverbial blunt instrument. And so another member of the crew was taken ashore for medical attention and shipped home. Lest the home office think that this procession of walking wounded would never stop, the Chief added an addendum to the report he sent to the superintendent engineer in Victoria.

"As you will know we have had some trouble with excessive drinking. This seems to be under control now, and I do not think we will have any more troubles once we are away from the fleshpots of Japan."

And so, before further accidents could befall them (or so they

The Ketchikan, *on her way to Prudhoe Bay, having dropped her load of logs and been reloaded with pipe.* Peter Davies photo

thought), they picked up their two loaded barges and headed toward the Aleutians. Both barges were carrying pipe and it had been loaded so far above the stanchions that chains had been fastened over the top of the load to hold it in place.

By July 9 they were well out in the Pacific. At 10:35 that evening the mate noticed a radar echo 1$^1/_2$ miles astern. He reduced speed and five minutes later the echo was 2 miles astern. "Suspect lost tow" he noted in the log, and went to call Buster.

It was confirmed, then: the towline had broken and the second barge, the *Ketchikan*, was drifting out in the dark, rough seas. The *Sudbury II* could do very little but wait for daylight. When it arrived the deck crew hauled in the first barge and discovered that the break had occurred just past the coupling to the second one. This meant that at the bow of the *Ketchikan*, 1,100 feet of 2-inch wire was hanging straight down into the depths.

In a 30-knot wind there was no way the *Sudbury II* dared approach the dead weight of the *Ketchikan*, but by July 13 the weather had moderated and by noon the deck crew had burnt off sections of broken chain, secured the first barge to a buoy and set it adrift. Now they turned their attention to the herculean task of hauling the *Ketchikan*'s pennant, literally tons of wire, up out of the water by hand until enough was on deck to secure to the capstan. The job was made more difficult by the steep swell still running. Only a mariner can truly grasp the difficulty of getting a 200-foot tug close to a 10,000-ton barge in a swell without doing serious damage to both vessels. As the deck crew laboured to get a wire around the bridle and pick up the pennant, the *Sudbury II* heaved and pitched and periodically crashed against the barge. Finally they got pickup lines on the pennant and attempted to pull some of it on deck. They had begun this struggle at noon; it was now almost 5:00 p.m.. They had worked without even a break for lunch and they were exhausted. Buster felt he must spell somebody off. The second mate, Jim Talbott, took over. "Jimmy, you handle her," said Buster. "Just keep the stern end up to the gear and I'll go back and see what I can do."

On the afterdeck there was a web of wires going to the capstan and the towing winch. Buster and John Kerr hung over the edge, got some straps on the wire and managed to stop it off. Then, suddenly, the two pickup lines carried away. Buster jumped back and his leg was caught between two parts of the stopper wire.

Always, on a ship like the *Sudbury II*, there lurks in the back of each man's mind the fear of injury. The work they did presented uncountable opportunities to get hurt. And *where* they worked—off the Aleutian Islands or 2,000 miles out in the Pacific—serious injury could mean death. Their only protection from this ever-present danger was superior seamanship, a cool head and luck. Now luck was on Buster Fransvaag's side; the wire that could have sliced off his leg in an instant didn't. It had ripped through his trousers and torn into his flesh, but because it wasn't under strain he remained intact.

The cool head belonged to Peter Davies. He was in the engine room when he was alerted to the first indication of trouble by the sudden appearance of the bosun.

"Buster's caught in the wire," he yelled and grabbed for the acetylene torch. In his haste he forgot that a cutting torch needs fuel. Peter turned on the acetylene bottles and sprinted after him. On deck he found Buster and a deckhand alone on the aft end, towing wire singing all around them. The deckhand was struggling to light the torch.

"I'll take it," said Peter, grabbing the torch and lighting it in one swift movement. He dropped onto his back on the deck, directed the torch's bright tongue of flame at the wire and it fell away.

Now, stumbling through the towing gear that littered the deck, crew members got a stretcher to Buster's side, heaved him onto it and moved him into his cabin—a task accomplished with some effort because their patient refused morphine and continued to try to direct operations. But this little MASH unit worked together in the medical emergency as well as they did as a towboat crew. They administered penicillin and what little painkiller Buster would accept and strapped up the wound. A jet of blood pulsated from the back of the skipper's leg, which worried Peter considerably, but lack of medical knowledge precluded any further remedies. Besides, the Chief's duties as first aid man were somewhat fragmented for he kept having to leave the patient to go down to check on what was happening in the engine room.

At this point in the *Sudbury II*'s log, mid-page, the handwriting suddenly changes. It is now the first mate, John Currie, who is in charge of the tug with her drifting barges and deck covered with towing wire. In a hurried scrawl he noted the time of the accident: 20:50. Within twenty minutes the deck crew had buoyed off the *Ketchikan*'s bridle and the *Sudbury II* was surging off at top speed into the gathering darkness leaving her two drifting barges behind her. In the pilothouse new courses were plotted that would take the ship to Kushiro, the nearest port city. As they drove through the night, anxious crew members checked the "Old Man" regularly. They had great respect for their captain and were deeply concerned about him, but all they could do was wipe his forehead and offer encouragement.

As they neared their destination the *Sudbury II*'s radio-telephone alerted those on shore, and in Kushiro there was a flurry as the harbour pilot, doctor and ambulance arrived in that order. It took four small Japanese ambulance attendants to transfer Buster's hulking frame to their vehicle. At the hospital a doctor examined him and then two nurses wheeled in a trolley with something that resembled a storage battery with two copper prongs on it. They started to cauterize the wound on Buster's leg and now, at last, he permitted himself the luxury of fainting.

A new captain, Tim Cary, flew out from Victoria, bringing with him a replacement for the non-cook, and the crew, thus augmented and immensely relieved to hear that Buster wouldn't lose his leg, headed back into the Pacific. Somewhere in its vast reaches drifted their barges of pipe. They had taken their position when they dropped the barges but either that position wasn't accurate, or the barges had drifted some considerable distance, or perhaps some attempt to tow them had been made. For when they finally did locate them with the aid of an aircraft and another big Japanese tug, the *Seiha Maru*, there were lines on them that had not been there when they left. Left unattended, the barges were theoretically salvage and no doubt their value had proved a temptation, but their size was their protection. Barges of this size were too much for most would-be salvagers to handle.

Now came the task of reconnecting the tow. Tim Cary, parachuted unexpectedly into this job, was operating under two handicaps. First, he had never captained the *Sudbury II* and had had virtually no time to familiarize himself with her; second, he had come aboard accompanied by Seaspan's port captain, a representative of Crowleys—the barges' owners—and a Japanese surveyor. All these gentlemen had advice and opinions to offer. It was suggested that a kedge anchor on the end of the towline could be used as a hook to snag the pennant. The *Sudbury II* approached the *Ketchikan*, paid out 800 feet of towline with the anchor attached and made several passes around the bow of the barge hoping to snag the pennant—without success. Then the *Seiha Maru* and the *Sudbury II*, with the weighted line between them, made a sweep of the *Ketchikan* from stern to bow, again without success. On the third attempt they paid out 300 feet of line and the kedge with a buoy attached to the line and circled the barge, an arrangement that proved equally fruitless. They lengthened the line to 800 feet with similar results. They had started all this at 5:00 a.m.; it was almost noon. Tim decided the time had come to exert his own authority. "You know, there's another way to do this," he said. "We've got this bloody great tug out here, this Japanese tug, and he's got a great big crew. He's here. We've hired him. Let's use him."

So the *Seiha Maru* launched her work boat, got a slip wire around the chain bridles of the *Ketchikan* and ran it to the *Sudbury II*'s stern. The tug hauled in a bight of the pennant and connected the towline to the pennant with a strap and roller shackle. Finally hooked up to the *Ketchikan*, they used the services of the motorboat to help them pick up the second barge. Then their three passengers reboarded the Japanese tug for the trip home via Japan, and by 4:20 p.m. the *Sudbury II* was full away for Prudhoe Bay—or so her captain supposed.

The weather was in their favour; for days the log recorded "slight sea, low swell." It was not until they were off Amchitka Pass that there was any intimation of further trouble. Then, in the early hours of July 28, the third engineer phoned up the bridge and asked, "What's happened?"

"Nothing's happened," was the reply. "Why?"

"All of our meters have just surged."

"No," said the bridge, "Both barges are still on the radar. Everything's fine."

To make doubly sure that it was, a deckhand went aft to check the towing gear, which settled the matter until first light. In the morning, however, the crew discovered that the tug did indeed have two barges behind her but that the stanchions on the starboard side of the larger barge had collapsed. The *Ketchikan* had dumped her load of pipe and had assumed a pronounced list to port. Everybody was on deck now, looking astern. And then, as they watched, the barge turned over very slowly until she was upside down with only her black bottom visible above the surface of the sea.

Tim Cary reduced speed and stationed a man at the winch brake. Then he sent out a stream of messages: to Red Stack in Seattle to advise them of the loss of cargo, to Adak Coast Guard requesting an assist tug, and to Seaspan in Vancouver. It was

The hull of the Ketchikan, *rising from the waters of the bay like a huge beached whale.* Peter Davies photo

now blowing northwest 30 to 35 knots. They were 22 miles east of East Cape, Amchitka Island.

For two days the *Sudbury II* dragged both barges toward Constantine Harbour and, day and night for those two days, a man stood by the winch brake. The condition of the *Ketchikan* appeared to be unchanged; a bubble of air inside her hull was keeping her afloat but it was not a situation anyone on the tug would take for granted. Now as they closed in on the harbour they considered another problem: Tim had no large-scale charts for it.

It was Fred Collins who came to their aid. Fred, seemingly unable to distance himself from this calamitous voyage, had already arrived by air. He placed heading markers at the harbour's entrance to guide her in and on the *Sudbury II*'s afterdeck the crew shortened the towline. By noon on July 30 the tug was tied to the dock with the upright barge alongside and the *Ketchikan* in the middle of the bay.

The sun that had heralded the day continued to shine and the spectacle of the Aleutians, as they appeared that day, remains a vivid memory. The sky was brilliant blue, snow-capped mountains rose in all directions and the islands, at their lower level, were lush green. But that was the only day, in the five weeks that the *Sudbury II* spent there, that offered such a view. The rest of the time it poured; it snowed; it was so foggy that the crew dared not leave the confines of the harbour for fear of getting lost.

Jack Daly, Island Tug's diver, had arrived with Fred Collins. He got an air hose under the barge and for hours the staccato sound of an air compressor echoed across the water. The black bulk of the *Ketchikan* rose 2 feet, but this was a mixed blessing: a 40-knot wind was blowing by now and this increased buoyancy increased the barge's capacity to drift. The *Sudbury II* started her engines and all night she pushed this monster away from the moored barge. It was with some anticipation, then, that she awaited the arrival of the American tug *Jupiter*, which had been rerouted with instructions to pick up the smaller barge and take it to its destination, Prudhoe Bay. The tug's appearance was more than welcome as far as Tim was concerned, but the American captain didn't share his feelings.

"Oh shit," he snarled at his dispatcher in Seattle. "We're on our way home and now you tell me we have to turn around and go back where we came from."

Fred Collins and Jack Daly were the first in a procession of people who began to descend upon the *Sudbury II*. Five divers came from Fred Devine's company in Astoria; extra crew members flew up from Victoria; underwriters and marine surveyors appeared. They filled every berth, ate quantities of food and used up the *Sudbury II*'s limited supply of water. Her engineers tried making fresh water with their evaporators but the exercise wasn't a great success, so they conferred and came up with another solution to the water problem. They dammed a little stream, put a fire pump in place and ran their fire hose to the vessel.

While these logistical problems were being solved, a squad of divers were swarming around, or rather under, the upturned *Ketchikan*, which lay in the harbour like a gigantic beached whale. Using underwater cutting equipment, they first removed all the barge's stanchions. Then, welding underwater, they made the hull and the bulkheads watertight and pumped more air into these cavities. With every day the barge rose higher out of the water and when it was considered sufficiently buoyant it was righted by means of a procedure called a parbuckle—all of which sounds very straightforward except for the fact that we're not discussing a bathtub toy here, but a 10,000-ton steel barge. Two cables were attached to the shore, run under both ends of the barge and secured on her far side. The *Sudbury II* positioned herself with her stern facing the midships portion of the barge's offshore side, and from her bow two anchors were dropped off her port and starboard sides and then buried deep in the harbour bottom by divers with high-pressure hoses. Their anchor chains were connected to wires which were pulled taut by the vessel's windlass. This ground tackle firmly in place, two wires were stretched from the towing winch on the afterdeck out and under both ends of the barge and secured on the sides opposite those from the shore. While all this rigging was taking place, water was pumped into the compartments on one side of the barge and air into those on the opposite side to provide a list. The tug, engines ahead, then heaved on her windlass and winch. There is always the danger, when exerting so much force, that tackle will break, and the backlash from a snapping cable is a lethal weapon. For moments, with engines pounding and cable singing with strain, everyone held their breath. But it worked, just as it was supposed to, and the *Ketchikan* was upright once more.

An unlikely partner in this endeavour was, of all things, the Atomic Energy Commission. In 1970 the Americans had exploded a nuclear device on this remote island and each summer scientists spent some time on Amchitka studying the effects of the explosion on the flora and fauna. There was a large airport on the island, and roads snaked here and there connecting a number of Quonset huts. More important to the *Sudbury II*, there was a warehouse containing pickup trucks, gasoline and supplies of all kinds. The

Atomic Energy Commission had given the salvage men access to this equipment, which helped enormously, as it allowed them to transport personnel, compressors, diving gear, steel plating and all manner of things from the airstrip to the harbour. Now the trucks were used to take this personnel and their equipment back to the airstrip for the return journey, via Reeves Air, to Anchorage and from there to Seattle. Meanwhile, in Victoria, a crew, headed by Captain John Webb was preparing to leave for Alaska, to relieve the *Sudbury II*'s crew and bring the *Ketchikan* back to its home port. René Fournier was going as Chief.

"We were called to leave Vancouver Airport at five o'clock; we were to go to Seattle in two separate aircraft. Nobody had told us where we were going, only that we were going north. Well, it turned out that one of the oilers was late so John Webb said, 'Well, you guys get on the first plane and when that guy gets here we'll all join up and catch the big plane from Seattle.' He gave us our tickets.

"We checked in at Seattle but the rest of the guys didn't show up. Time came and we got on the plane and off we went. We saw their plane taxiing in as we were taking off but oh well, what the hell, what can you do?"

Milling around in the Anchorage airport, they realized that their captain, the only member of the crew who knew where they were going, was still en route. They had no idea of their destination. René got to a phone and called Victoria.

"Oh, thank God you called," said the man in personnel. "There are people looking all over for you up there. They're carrying signs around. Didn't you see them?"

"Sure," said René. "There's people all over the place waving signs saying Amchitka. How are we supposed to know what Amchitka means? We thought they were Jesus freaks."

So René went up to one of the placard-bearers. "We're the guys you're looking for."

"Oh god. The plane's leaving in ten minutes." The man rushed them all to the head of the line, elbowing the less fortunate passengers out of the way.

"These are the men I've been looking for," he said to the ticket clerk, and there was a flurry of ticket stamping.

They clambered onto the plane to Amchitka with moments to spare and off they went into the wild foggy yonder. As if all this flying around weren't novelty enough for a bunch of towboaters, at their destination they were introduced to another new experience: the "fighter pilot" approach. Their plane skimmed in just over the water, went up and over the land mass and, since the airstrip was visible, it landed. Otherwise it would have kept right on going. René explained the modus operandi: "This airline just goes back and forth across the Aleutian chain. If they can land someplace they land. If they can't, they carry their load all the way back and they just keep recirculating until the day comes when they can drop it in." This system became crystal clear as days went by and John Webb's group failed to show up. Eight days later they appeared. Each day they had gone out and climbed aboard the plane; each day they landed at every other stop on the Aleutian chain; each day they were prevented from landing in Amchitka by the weather. "But they visited every place in the Aleutian chain," said René. "They had a hell of a good time."

CHAPTER XV

The Corinna

"All the Canadian naval personnel on the West Coast followed with interest and admiration the saga of your recent rescue of the SS Corinna.*"*

In 1975, on Father's Day, Harold Elworthy died, and the last link with the *Sudburys*' glory days was broken. The *McCurdy Marine History of the Pacific Northwest* recorded his passing: "Harold B. Elworthy, 74, one of British Columbia's best known and most respected shipping men, died at Victoria." A few months before his death, however, the *Sudbury II*, as if to prove to H.B. that she still had it in her, went out and rescued the *Corinna*.

The tug had just arrived in Port Alberni with a paper barge that she had towed from San Francisco. It was Christmas Eve 1974 and her crew had many and various plans for the holidays. The *Sudbury II*'s captain, Frank Culbard, was taking off for

Hawaii; her first mate, Suraj Gulati, had two months' holiday coming to him; her Chief Engineer, Harry Sapro, would celebrate with his wife and two small daughters. But just hours before they were to leave for Victoria, Frank Culbard received a message requesting him to go to the assistance of a disabled ship, and all holiday plans were put on hold. A thousand miles out in the Gulf of Alaska, the Liberian freighter *Corinna* had sent out a distress call. A week earlier she had lost her boilers, and since then she had wallowed in frighteningly heavy seas while her engineers made futile efforts to effect emergency repairs. She had no power, no heat, no lights. She was 500 feet long but the mountainous seas rolled her almost onto her side and pounded her so severely that her plumbing fixtures shattered. "It was very, very rough," said her radio operator later. "Our ship was something like a twisted thing." The captain rationed his food supplies, handed out a daily tot of liquor and waited anxiously for a rescuer.

Five days after the *Corinna*'s breakdown, the first help appeared on the horizon: the US Coast Guard cutter *Confidence*, explosions of spray bursting over her bows. In the huge seas that crashed over both ships there was nothing the cutter could do but stand off. The two vessels could communicate by radio, however, and anticipating the arrival of a tug, the cutter's captain inquired about emergency power to the winches.

Yes, they did have an emergency diesel generator, came the reply. But when they started it, it had shut down and couldn't be restarted.

"Automatic shutdown," muttered the Coast Guard engineer standing at the captain's elbow.

"You want to go over there and get it going?" inquired his captain.

For days the wind had blown at Force 11 but there are lulls in even the most violent and prolonged storms. Now came one of these pauses. The wind dropped. Big seas streaked with foam still heaved by, but with less wind to catch her bulk, the *Corinna* was drifting more slowly and her lee side offered some shelter. The cutter's captain decided to take a chance. If he could get a couple of his engineers on board perhaps they could get some power to the deck winch. He was willing to try, and so were two engineers.

The *Confidence*'s deck crew bunched her fenders on her starboard quarter and the *Corinna*'s crew dropped a rope ladder down their ship's side. Then the engineers inched their way forward, clinging to the rails; beside them two members of the deck crew clutched life rings on heaving lines as backup should they miss the ladder. Now the captain brought the *Confidence* in at a 45-degree angle. Ten feet from the towering hull of the *Corinna*, a wave threw her against solid steel; the bulwarks buckled and the fenders groaned. Ignoring his ship's protests, the captain lunged along the hull to the ladder and the first crewman jumped. Clinging like a limpet to the swinging ladder, he paused for a moment—but only for a moment: the cutter, having dropped into the trough, now rose like an elevator and chased him briskly upwards. For two or three minutes the *Corinna* had rolled away from the cutter. This movement now reversed itself, and she began rolling down on top of the smaller ship. The *Confidence*, her engines full astern, made her escape. Then, timing the rolls, the captain went in again; the second man jumped, grasped the rungs securely, and there was a collective sigh of relief as the cutter dropped into a trough and got well away.

Down in the black depths of the *Corinna*'s engine room, the two Coast Guard men shone their lights around, looking for the diesel generator. The ship was still rolling horribly. Under their feet the oily metal deck canted steeply, first in one direction and then in the opposite, so that they were either clawing their way upward or clinging to some handhold to avoid sliding downward. Despite these less than ideal working conditions they found the engine they were looking for, searched under the deck plates for valves, checked oil and fuel pressure and restarted it. Now there were a few dim lights on board and enough electricity to run a winch. The men's reward for this heroic effort was an extended stay on the *Corinna*. It had taken exceptional seamanship to get them aboard; by the time they were ready to leave, it was impossible for them to do so. For two days they waited for the seas to moderate enough to permit the perilous trip back to the cutter. Now both ships waited for further help to arrive.

In Port Alberni the *Sudbury II*'s crew abandoned their hopes for Christmas ashore without complaint. Terry Garraghan, the cook, took stock of his depleted supplies and made out order forms. Harry Sapro, the Chief, supervised the fuelling of the tug's twenty-six fuel tanks. And then, in the darkness of the afternoon of December 24, the tug turned on her heel and barrelled down the Alberni "canal," which isn't really a canal but rather a long, narrow inlet that extends from the Pacific Ocean deep into the heart of Vancouver Island. At dinner, the slow rise and fall of the *Sudbury II*'s bows told those in the windowless mess room that they had left sheltered waters and were out in the open Pacific.

By the time they reached the northern tip of Vancouver Island, gusts of wind were rattling the *Sudbury II*'s rigging, the groundswell was replaced by short steep seas and a sleety rain slanted out of the overcast sky. Frank Culbard thought longingly of Hawaii.

And in the galley Terry Garraghan began his preparations for Christmas dinner. If fortune had robbed the *Sudbury II*'s crew of their holiday festivities, it had, at least, provided them with an outstanding cook. Terry Garraghan, small and wiry, is a professionally trained chef who first went to sea during World War II. At fourteen he was mess boy on the run to Murmansk—a stretch of ocean so fraught with danger that only a few of the merchant ships that left England actually arrived there. The captain of Terry's ship, not happy about exposing this child to the very real possibility of death, suggested to Terry that he leave the ship and seek a safer livelihood. Terry ignored the suggestion. Leaving his ship and his shipmates wouldn't have entered his mind. He remained where he was and later, when the crew went off to Buckingham Palace to receive medals from the King, he was there to receive his. After the war he had worked his way up in the catering department of ocean liners. His standards were high and the holiday dinner he served was complete with all the trimmings.

If the weather off the northern tip of Vancouver Island was "snarly," the weather in the Gulf of Alaska was horrendous. Still hundreds of miles from her quarry, the *Sudbury II* battered her way northward through mountainous seas and storm-force winds. Her speed had been reduced to 8 knots and some of the crew had serious doubts about a safe return. "We've got to be short on brains to be out here in this," they agreed.

For his part, Terry had moved to a berth below decks. In his own cabin the noise of the seas roaring down the decks made it impossible to sleep. "It sounded like being in a tunnel with a train going through," he remembers.

The winds were gusting at over 100 miles per hour; in the trough the tops of the waves, level with the crossbars of the mast, blotted out the rest of the world. Frank Culbard searched his memory. "I can only think of one other time I've been out in seas like these," he told the struggling helmsman, "and that was rounding Cape Horn on the *City of Alberni*."

Finally, just before nightfall on Sunday, December 29, the *Sudbury II* spotted the *Corinna*. It was snowing but the wind had dropped. A huge groundswell lifted the ships up on the crests of the waves and dropped them into the troughs, so the *Sudbury II* kept her distance. If either ship had slid down one of these waves into the other the rescue would have been over before it started.

"I want you at the controls in the engine room," the skipper told his Chief. "I won't use the telegraph and I won't give you much warning."

Harry Sapro had been with the *Sudbury II* for eight years. For him, her complex diesel-electric power plant was a challenge he enjoyed. With the enthusiasm of a research scientist he had analyzed the engines' idiosyncrasies and found solutions to their problems. He had installed larger fuel filters to reduce clogging and had isolated the fuel lines so when they vibrated they wouldn't contact another surface and crack. And in seas like these he left the plugs slack in the cooling water lines so that when they got air-locked the air could escape. Despite all this expertise, those in the engine room were battling a host of problems. The days when no expense on maintenance was spared were over; the *Sudbury II* was long overdue for an overhaul. Keeping these tired engines running in a hurricane required effort, ingenuity and a touch of genius. The Chief and his engineers supplied it. As John Rodgers had pointed out twelve years before, "Losing power under such conditions was unthinkable." They had no intention of letting this happen.

So, in the engine room, Harry stood poised and ready to respond to the orders that came down the voice pipe: "Slow ahead—gimme a little more—that's too much—" and on the afterdeck a little knot of men watched nervously as the *Corinna*'s towering bow drifted down on them, rising and falling, cleaving the water like a monstrous saw. As it slid past them John Kendall, the *Sudbury II*'s bosun, fired the rocket gun. He had never handled a rocket gun before but his first attempt was a great success: it curved toward the *Corinna*, landed on her deck and was seized by anxious pairs of hands. Entertaining some hope that their ordeal would eventually be over, brought the *Corinna*'s exhausted crew new energy—which was just as well, because now they had to haul in the first light lines by hand, and then the dead weight of the towing wire with a little windlass powered by the diesel generator. It took a couple of hours of back-breaking work to haul in the wire and secure it to the anchor chain, but once that was accomplished the US Coast Guard cutter felt it safe to leave the scene.

For ten days, in screaming winds and in seas so huge that they battered the clocks and fans from the *Corinna*'s bulkheads, the *Confidence* had stood by, her very presence sustaining those on the crippled ship. The fact that the cutter, a small symbol of the world's largest democracy, was there for a Red Chinese merchantman, wasn't lost on any of the parties. Nor did it diminish the *Corinna*'s captain's gratitude. "I can't thank you enough," Captain Jung Wen-Wang radioed to the departing *Confidence*. "Happy New Year and God bless you all. Again, God bless you all."

Now the *Sudbury II* set a course for Cape Flattery and commenced her tow. As if on cue the wind, which had dropped while the towline was being connected, descended upon the two ships with full ferocity. Struggling through monstrous waves, the tow almost invisible behind them, they made no progress but simply held their own. And suddenly they weren't even doing that: a gigantic wave threw the *Corinna* on her beam ends and broke the towline. Once again the freighter was drifting helplessly, rolling so wildly that no one aboard dared to go on deck.

"Unmitigated shit," said Frank Culbard. "I know damn well what the problem is," he told his Chief at breakfast. "That guy didn't put out enough chain." As was usual in such a situation, the *Sudbury II* had used the freighter's anchor chain as a bridle. Its weight held it down under the surface of the water and its belly provided a "spring" for the towing wire itself—or this would have been the case had enough chain been let out. Frank's radio conversation with the *Corinna*'s captain left him with the distinct suspicion that the tow's deck crew had only let out half the chain specified.

Harry Sapro helped himself to a little more bacon. "Some people don't do what they're told," he said.

The seas were too big to attempt a reconnection. Instead *Sudbury II* "stood by"—a passive-sounding term that couldn't begin to describe the conditions she was enduring. The seas that were sweeping over her left all her forward rails and the bulkhead in front of the wheelhouse bent onto the deck itself. In weather such as this some cooks resort to sandwiches, but in the *Sudbury II*'s galley the spirit of Murmansk prevailed. Terry Garraghan would have none of this sandwich idea. "Some people say, 'I can't do this; it's too bad out there.' They give in. I won't give in. The crew are entitled to full meals. That's what I'm there for." So in the galley, in a hurricane, he was preparing a five-course New Year's dinner, because at New Year's, "they expect a little bit something extra, you know." The menu read:

Hors D'Oeuvre

Soupe de Champignon
Salmon Vol-au-Vent
Savory Stuffed Green Peppers

Roast Turkey
Cranberry Sauce
Chipolata
Parsnips–Green Peas–Finger Carrots
Creamed Potatoes–Potatoes Bercy

Steamed Fruit Pudding with Rum Sauce
Strawberry Cream Slick Cake
Assorted Nuts–Candies

Beverages by Seaspan

At the top of the menu was the notation: "At Sea North Pacific. Towing disabled freighter *Corinna*."

The *Sudbury II* was rolling to 56 degrees. To cook such a meal under those conditions seems unbelievable. To eat it presented difficulties as well; like human gimbals the crew held onto their crockery with one hand and ate with the other. The fact that they still had appetites is equally awe-inspiring. "You could turn a ship upside down and I'd still be at the table," said Harry Sapro.

The Liberian freighter Corinna, *January 2, 1975. The* Sudbury II *had towed her through mountainous seas and storm-force winds.*
Captain Frank Culbard photo, Seaspan

For more than twenty-four hours the *Sudbury II* kept track of her charge in the chaos that enveloped both vessels. Then, at 2:00 a.m. on January 2, in a blinding snowstorm, the wind abated. Once more the tug sidled up to the *Corinna*; once more John Kendall fired a rocket and once more it reached its target on the first try. Once more the weary Chinese grappled with wire that weighed 11 pounds a foot. And this time Frank Culbard made sure his instructions were followed to the letter.

While all this was taking place on deck, Terry Garraghan had other things in mind. He was busy in the galley preparing a CARE parcel. He knew from radio communications with the *Corinna* that her crew had been on reduced rations for days so Terry, with cultural preferences in mind, raided his larder and prepared a 100-pound plastic-wrapped box containing fish, rice and chickens. He attached a note that read: "From the crew of the *Sudbury II*, a gift to the crew of the SS *Corinna*." The whole thing was placed in a netting bag and hauled across from the tug to the freighter.

Now the wind came howling down upon them again, the strongest gusts measuring 105 miles an hour. "Try to imagine," a crew member said, "the room you are in heaving up and tilting over at a 45-degree angle. You grab for something to hang onto. Then it tilts over in the opposite direction. Now imagine that happening for thirty hours at a stretch."

Every twenty-four hours a deckhand threw the whole weight of his body against a door and fought his way outside. As he made his way aft to grease the fairlead and change the nip in the towline, the wind ripped at his clothes and numbing sea water rushed past his legs.

In the engine room it was at least warm and dry, if not stationary. Harry Sapro worked his way around the engines looking for fuel leaks, listening for unusual noises, checking gauges. Harry is a man of ample girth and phlegmatic temperament. He *likes* engines, and he confronted the complex and aging machinery on the *Sudbury II* with an air of stolid confidence. Before the *Corinna*'s rescue he had brushed off the suggestion that the Cooper-Bessemers were getting to the end of the road. "I could keep those engines running forever," he said. And he had certainly proved his case out in the Gulf of Alaska.

On January 6 the *Sudbury II* entered the port of Vancouver, the *Corinna* looming behind her on a short line. Twenty years before, in December 1955, the newspapers announced the SS *Sudbury*'s triumphant return with the *Makedonia*, in headlines an inch and a half high. "EPIC SEA FIGHT IN PICTURES" screamed the

The Sudbury II *towing the* Corinna *into Vancouver Harbour.* Vancouver Maritime Museum

front page of the *Vancouver Sun*. In contrast to this, in January 1975 the Victoria *Times* stated of the *Corinna*'s successful rescue, "There was no fanfare as the *Sudbury II* slipped into her berth in the Inner Harbour this morning."

In one respect nothing had changed. The *Sudbury II*'s achievement was no less than that of the SS *Sudbury*. The rescue of the *Corinna* required the same outstanding seamanship and the same fortitude as the rescue of the *Makedonia*. The changes that had occurred were changes in ownership, management style and economic conditions. This time the harbour wasn't cleared of traffic, no car horns blared, there were no bonuses to be handed out.

The crew weren't looking for glory, but they *were* looking for recognition. "I was disappointed," said Terry Garraghan. "When we got back one of the big noises came over and said, 'Oh, you're going to be well paid,' but we didn't get an extra *nickel*. And when we got back I thought they'd say, 'Right-o, they brought the boat in, now let's get the guys home.' But they didn't. They said, 'We're going to fuel up now' and we had about six hours doing this or that before we could go home. Everybody was really upset."

FROM: REAR-ADMIRAL R. JOHN PICKFORD, CD

THE COMMANDER MARITIME FORCES PACIFIC
FORCES MAIL OFFICE, VICTORIA, B.C.

8 January, 1975

Captain Frank Culbard
Ocean Tug SUDBURY II
c/o SEASPAN International Ltd
345 Harbour
Victoria, BC

Dear Captain Culbard:

All Canadian naval personnel on the West Coast followed with interest and admiration the saga of your recent rescue of the S.S. CORINNA. Your outstanding seamanship and determination to save life and property at sea in the face of appalling weather conditions sets a shining example for all of us to follow and is in the highest tradition of those who go down to the sea in ships.

Please accept for yourself, and convey to your crew, the admiration of officers, men and women of this Command and accept my congratulations on a job well done.

Sincerely,

R. J. Pickford

R. John Pickford
Rear-Admiral

Admiral Pickford's letter of commendation to the Sudbury II*'s Captain Culbard.* Courtesy Terry Garraghan

The men who had saved the *Corinna* had displayed just as much skill and courage as their predecessors, their efforts bringing a commendation from the navy's Rear Admiral, but their successful rescue was not the making of their company as the SS *Sudbury*'s had been. It was simply a reminder that the *Sudbury II* was still around draining the finances of her present owners.

In the 1950s and 1960s the *Sudbury*s and their crews went out repeatedly into some of the bleakest and most terrifying waters in the world. And for the first few years, at least, they were winging it all the way. Ship masters became boat handlers and learned to manouevre the *Sudbury*s with consummate skill under the most difficult conditions: towboaters learned how to find a dot in the Pacific that was another tug and then switch tows; twenty-year-olds learned to be engineers, working with one hand and hanging on with the other while their engine room threatened to roll over on them.

George Matson said, "Those guys didn't know a damned thing about this kind of thing until the *Makedonia*. They taught themselves—and they never lost a tow."

René Fournier said proudly, "As far as long-range towing on steel went we were as good as the best in the world."

But now, in the 1970s, the unique set of circumstances that required and rewarded such efforts had evaporated. There were no longer armadas of naval vessels heading for the scrap dealers in Japan. The rusty hulks that had survived the war and the hastily built Libertys that had helped to win it had been replaced by newer, more reliable ships whose state-of-the-art navigational equipment made the *Glafkos*'s simple compass seem pathetic. Stricter government regulations kept the hopelessly dilapidated out of the shipping lanes and for twenty-four hours a day Coast Guard employees sat at consoles and swept the coast with their electronic eyes, monitoring every ship in the area. Even in Europe the change was felt. The drop in business caused the two great Dutch salvage companies—Smit and Wijsmuller, competitors for a hundred years—to amalgamate and sell off many of their tugs.

There were still disasters, of course, despite all the precautions and improvements, but they were few. Any of the powerful new tugs could do what the *Sudburys* had done, and furthermore they could do it with fewer men. The *Sovereign*, the next largest tug in the Seaspan fleet, operated with a crew of eight as against the *Sudbury II*'s sixteen.

The figures were damning. During the whole of 1972, for example, the *Sudbury II* only worked a total of 181 days. In that year 5 percent of her time was spent on salvage work, 45 percent on commercial towing and the remaining 50 percent on station or being repaired. Even tied to the dock she cost the company a thousand dollars a day. And the repair bills from the Point Ellice Shipyards kept rolling in:

Number 2 piston disintegrated	$ 2,252.28
Strip down generator	1,260.89
Dismantle tow winch spooling carriage & remove diamond shaft dog	3,559.78
Main Engine repairs	8,014.79

There was no way out. In April 1979, *Sudbury II* was sold to I.D. Logan of Seattle for conversion to an offshore fishing and processing vessel. Just three years later, on October 31, 1982, she burned and sank in Hecate Strait.

Those who had sailed on her felt a blow to the pit of their stomachs. Their feelings couldn't be governed by a financial statement, for they had faced the worst the Pacific could deliver in this ship and she had brought them safely home. She is still mourned by those knew her. Her faults are overlooked, blurred by the indulgence of affection, and her legendary qualities are remembered.

Adrian Bull, one of her captains, said of one bad day in the Pacific, "It was just white out there; you couldn't see anything. We were taking seas right over the wheelhouse. I really loved that boat in the sense of being a sea boat. I'd go anywhere in that boat. I'm not worried about it. Just batten it down and let her go. [These] are wonderful sea boats. You don't appreciate that until you get on some of these other boats. It was a terrible ending for her. She deserved better."

The *Sudburys* are gone. They disappeared as quickly as they had come. They are gone and the adventure is over. All that is left are four plaques solidly embedded in the stone balustrade that skirts the Inner Harbour in Victoria. They read:

J.A. (Jack) Daly
Renowned Deep Sea Diver
From 1942–1977
Victoria, BC

Norman James Turner
1899–1980
Born at Nanoose Bay, Vancouver Island
Marine Surveyor, Salvage Master
and Engineer of International Repute

William Harley Blagborne
Master Mariner
Salvage Vessels
Sudbury and Sudbury II
1955–1964

Harold Barrington Elworthy
1901–1975
Native Son of Victoria
Founder of Island Tug & Barge Ltd.
Pioneering local, coastwise & deep sea towing & salvage
Philanthropist & leader in civic & maritime affairs

These small bronze rectangles confirm that there was once a company called Island Tug & Barge, run by a remarkable man whose initials, H.B., gave him his nickname, Hard-Boiled. The plaques also honour some of the many exceptional men H.B. employed. Capable and confident, they went out on these two ships and did their job—a job that sure beats the hell out of what most of us do for a living.

Index

T